# Vancouver's Hoboes

# VANCOUVER'S HOBOES

## Andrew Roddan

**SUB WAY**

**VANCOUVER**

Introduction © 2005 by Todd McCallum

**Library and Archives Canada Cataloguing in Publication**

Roddan, Andrew, d. 1948
    Vancouver's hoboes / Andrew Roddan ; introduction by Todd McCallum.
Originally published under title: God in the jungles.
ISBN 0-9687163-9-3
1. Tramps--British Columbia--Vancouver--History--20th century.
2. Homelessness--British Columbia--Vancouver--History--20th century. 3.
Church work with the homeless--British Columbia--Vancouver--History--
20th century. I. Roddan, Andrew, d. 1948 God in the jungles. II. Title.

HV4510.V35R62 2004              305.5'68
C2004-906165-8

Subway Books Ltd.
1819 Pendrell Street, Unit 203
Vancouver, B.C. V6G 1T3 Canada
Website: *www.subwaybooks.com*
E-mail: *subway@interlog.com*

Design and production: Jen Hamilton

Cover: Andrew Roddan (back panel, centre, without hat) distributing food at a
Vancouver hobo jungle, 1931. Photo by W.J. Moore. City of Vancouver Archives
RE N4.4, used by permission.

The publisher gratefully acknowledges the support of the Centre for Labour
Studies, Simon Fraser University.

Canadian orders:
Customer Order Department
University of Toronto Press Distribution
5201 Dufferin Street
Toronto, Ontario M3H 5T8

US orders:
University of Toronto Press Distribution
2250 Military Road
Tonawanda, New York 14150
Tel: (716) 693-2768
Fax: (716) 692-7479

Toll-free ordering from Canada or the US:
Tel: 1-800-565-9523
Fax: 1-800-221-9985
Email: *utpbooks@utpress.utoronto.ca*

# Contents

# Introduction

The businessman who suffers severe financial setbacks is of course a stock character in the popular mythology of the Great Depression. Such stories were indeed all too common in the 1930s. Yet the case of George Buscombe was special. A noted importer and exporter in Vancouver, Buscombe awoke one morning in the summer of 1931 to learn that one of his empty warehouses had vanished. The Union Street building had been "almost completely torn down," he complained to city officials, and the pieces spirited away somewhere; only the concrete foundation remained. Recounting the incident, Buscombe was reduced to musing on the obvious: "Happening in the heart of the city it is almost incredible," he said.

Was the building's disappearance evidence of organized crime in Vancouver's construction industry or the result of a natural disaster, perhaps an earthquake? No. Buscombe's investigations exposed an audacious plan executed by groups of homeless men who used the building's corrugated iron walls to construct two "hobo jungles," the makeshift communities devised by the jobless during the Depression and described as follows by Andrew Roddan:

> They may be found in clumps of wild bushes or among the trees, on the side of a stream, by the side of the road, near the railroad tracks, or in a disused lumber camp or factory. They are to be found in Australia, India, Japan, and in Great Britain as well as in Canada and America. Look at the picture and you will see that this jungle is composed of crude shelters made out of old tins, boards, boxes, disused motorcars, anything and everything, gathered from the dump heap nearby and formed into a rough shelter into which crawl, not animals, but homeless men, without saying their prayers, feeling as the Psalmist felt when he said: "No man careth for my soul." Their bellies slack and gnawing with hunger, they lie down and go to sleep, while the other half sleep in hotels and comfortable homes.

The quotation is from Roddan's *God in the Jungles*, written while he and others from First United Church, located at the corner of Gore and Hastings, mobilized to serve meals to thousands of homeless men that summer. As the person most associated in the public's mind with the homeless and their makeshift settlements, Roddan became the face of private charity in Depression-era Vancouver.

Although the Great Crash of October 1929 revealed the vulnerabilities of the Canadian economy, many initially thought that the loss of hundreds of thousands of jobs in the two subsequent years was a temporary downturn, a normal part of the business cycle. Only in mid-1931, with the dramatic growth of hobo jungles right "in the heart of the city," would Vancouver residents begin to use the term "the Depression". The two jungles implicated in the theft of the Buscombe warehouse—one on the False Creek flats near the Great Northern Railway terminal, the other along the shore of Burrard Inlet—were the smallest of the four jungles within the city limits, each housing between 150 and 200 persons. Another 250 men, most of them at least 40 years old, lived in a temporary structure built under the Georgia Viaduct. The fourth jungle, adjacent to Prior Street, housed approximately 450, most of them of Swedish and Finnish descent. Unknown numbers also squatted in Stanley Park, on Deadman's Island, and on the former Kitsilano reserve, the present Vanier Park.

*God in the Jungles* was published in 1931 by First United itself but has been out of print until now, when we have decided to reissue it under a more informative title. The next year, there was a follow-up volume, *Canada's Untouchables*, which was largely a rehash but with a harder edge. In both publications, Roddan offered an incisive and at times caustic critique of the failures of capitalism as revealed by the jungles' very existence. To demonstrate the mass devastation wrought by greed, he fixed on the hoboes who were forced by economic need to live in physical and moral degradation and whose stories, made public in *God in the Jungles*, eptomised the crisis, as much spiritual as economic, that plagued the western world. Roddan's message was one of redemption. Universal salvation was possible, he preached; even the degenerate tramp could be saved.

Hoboes were a necessary by-product of Confederation: as long as railway politics were the nation's politics, so too would those who built the railways (and those who bummed rides on them) take centre stage. From the 1870s to the 1930s, North America was home to a highly differentiated lot of wanderers who drifted in and out of unskilled jobs in logging, construction, stevedoring and other industries. Chicago was the so-called Main Stem of an elaborate network of railways crisscrossing the continent, built by masses of itinerants who used these products of their labour to travel thousands of miles in search of work, sociability, support and community. Chicago also gave birth to classification systems designed to come to terms with the realities of life on the road. Ben Reitman, America's self-proclaimed King of the Hoboes (and most famous as one of Emma Goldman's lovers), suggested that there are "three types of the genus vagrant, the hobo, the tramp and the bum. The hobo works and wanders, the tramp dreams and wanders and the bum drinks and wanders." Nicholas Klein, one-time president of Hobo College in Chicago, sounded a warning to those who would confuse these distinct groups:

> A hobo is one who travels in search of work, the migratory worker who must go about to find employment [....] The tramp is one who travels but does not work, and a bum is a man who stays in one place and does not work. Between these grades there is a great gulf of social distinction. Don't get tramps and hobos [sic] mixed. They are quite different in many respects. The chief difference being that the hobo will work and the tramp will not, preferring to live on what he can pick up at back doors as he makes his way through the country.

This system of classification became the standard. Nels Anderson adopted it with few modifications in his groundbreaking work of participant-observer sociology, *The Hobo*. The crisis of the 1930s, however, would shatter these neat categories. With mass unemployment, even people willing to work could not prevent long periods of idleness. Hoboes, in this sense, became tramps and bums of necessity.

Barry Broadfoot, the author of *Ten Lost Years*, perhaps the most compelling Canadian book on the 1930s, called the decade "the most traumatic in our nation's history, the most debilitating, the most devastating, the most horrendous." Less than a year after the Great Crash, H.W. Cooper, who as Vancouver's "relief officer" was in charge of such matters, complained that there "cannot be less than 10,000" unemployed men and women in the city, which as a traditional resting point for migrant workers naturally saw more than its share of "boxcar tourists" throughout the 1930s. In addition to the network of hotels, restaurants, flophouses and pool rooms geared to serving working people during the winter off-season, Vancouver was also home to numerous organisations offering transients material support and social contact. In 1931, thousands passed through the city—police constables reported 75 to 100 men arriving every day—prompting city council to warn Prime Minister R.B. Bennett that "the situation in Vancouver is beyond our control."

While makeshift settlements had existed in parts of Vancouver since the Crash, their size and scope expanded dramatically in 1931 because of worsening economic conditions, exacerbated by the Relief department's decision to slash 2,500 single male transients from the rolls that March. "It is estimated that 50 per cent of those cut off are still in the City," Cooper reported. With little possibility of work and now no possibility of municipal relief, homeless men worked in groups to construct their jungles and search for sustenance. Sydney Hutcheson, who wandered throughout British Columbia during the mid-1930s, believed that mutual assistance was one of the realities of the tramping life. "A man needed company at a time like this," he recalled, "as we had to stick together to live." According to available reports, each day one or two hoboes would head out to scrounge either food or money through a combination of begging, working and stealing, with the results being used to feed the group. While far from harmonious, jungle life was predicated on reciprocity in the distribution of food, drink, cigarettes and other goods. For a small gift of food, one could draw on the services of lawyers, doctors, dentists and barbers who were also on the bum. Jungles thus allowed the homeless to live a relatively autonomous existence, free from the prying eyes of social workers.

Like the transients to whom he ministered, Roddan was a newcomer to Vancouver. Born in Hawick, Scotland, in 1882, he was, among other things, a lay missionary with the Royal Navy before arriving in Canada in 1910. He completed studies at the University of Manitoba before beginning his first field mission, and spent nine years as minister of Winnipeg's Home Street Presbyterian and another three at St. Paul's United in Port Arthur, Ontario. He had come to Vancouver only as recently as December 1929 to take charge of First United's outpost on the edge of skid row.

His background as an apprentice to Salem Bland marked him as proponent of what was known as the Social Gospel, a movement that sought to make the church relevant to the real world by relieving the suffering engendered by, in this case, the new economic problems. He stood out by championing First United as the "Church of the Open Door," home to "27 different nationalities" worshipping together in a true demonstration of tolerance. He also preached a critique of the materialism that had dominated the 1920s. He possessed an evangelical awareness of the importance of the "industrial question" to the church's mission. Engagement was one of the Social Gospel's central pillars, and in time he would come to chastise fellow churchgoers, especially those in wealthier neighbourhoods, for their failure to act charitably towards the unemployed. At one point, he even suggested that the church "has shown little interest in [the homeless] apart from the fact that some church members may have invested their money in the project on which they are working, and they are looking for the dividends in return." His campaign for poor-relief, then, looked to alleviate suffering and to impel others to genuine acts of Christian charity. Looked at another way, the masses of the homeless and the hungry were a market niche serviced by no other institution, First United being one of only two citizens' groups contributing to municipal relief.

Roddan was gifted with a flamboyant speaking style and was a popular radio personality. This further increased his prominence and was valuable to the relief effort. One female parishioner claimed that "people responded splendidly to Mr. Roddan's appeals over the radio, great quantities of food being received and the workers were proud and grateful to be able to participate in such a beneficent and Christ-like work." Yet clearly Roddan was not alone in this effort, which required dozens of volunteer labourers. One of the most important was Jeannie MacDuff, "the Pin-Up Girl for the Hungry and Homeless" who ran First United's soup kitchen and served 1,252 patrons in a single sitting in November 1930. But in a photograph of Roddan in front of the crowd that record-breaking day, she is nowhere to be seen. MacDuff later recalled that she and her fellow volunteers put "something personal [into] every bowl of soup we handed to a hungry man. We tried to make each man feel he was somebody pretty important." She "never heard a complaint" from her colleagues in the kitchen: "The stove was hot and the sweat poured from our faces but it was as though we were all one big family." Such women's labour provided the foundation for Roddan's mission in the jungles.

By providing "flesh and blood" sketches of the homeless, Roddan in his two books hoped to convince the federal government to assume responsibility for the transients. His account blended personal stories gathered in the jungles with material from a variety of other sources. For example, some of the section titles in *God in the Jungles* and indeed even some of the narrative were lifted from *The Hobo*, Nels Anderson's work about the so-called Hobohemia of Chicago in 1921-22. Such practices make it difficult for readers to ascertain what material Roddan drew from his personal encounters and what was taken from other sources, even though some of the latter contradicted his message. Nonetheless we should appreciate Roddan's account of the jungles in the context of its explicitly salvationist message: these were tramps as seen through the eyes of one seeking to redeem their souls by rescuing them from sinful poverty.

In arguing for the potential redemption of the transients, he was taking up a lonely position. Most other writers believed tramps were subhuman, "the scum of Europe," as one ex-soldier put it, "almost entirely under the influence of these Communistic Leaders." A doctor opined that the jobless were in danger of becoming "degenerates of the worst kind [...] if surplus energy is not worked off." Even Roddan was not free of such stereotypes:

> Here, in this class, you will find the drug addicts, coke eaters, alcoholics, moral perverts, morons, feeble-minded, canned-heat artists, and if there be any other class or type of depraved humanity, you can put them in this category [....] When day after day as the bread line passes by, you learn to pick them out by their bleary eyes, shaky hands, trembling bodies, unkempt appearance, dirty clothes, gabbling tongues, always grousing about something or somebody, or sullen, morose and quiet. In this class we find ourselves face to face with the human derelict [....] They are at the bottom of the scale, some of them lower than the beasts of the fields.

This passage has a timeless quality. It could have been written about the poor of London's East End by one of a thousand of mid-Victorian moralists. Nor does it strike our present-day sensibilities as particularly graphic, as it was meant to be in 1931. One could, I believe, successfully pass it off as a quote about street people taken from a riding association newsletter for a member of Premier Gordon Campbell's government. "My community has suffered awful, awful atrocities" at the hands of so-called street people, Lorne Mayencourt, the MLA for the riding of Vancouver-Burrard, said in May 2004, when he thus became the latest public figure to make political hay with a proposal to criminalise panhandling in the name of public safety.

What makes Roddan's image of absolute degradation different was the fact that it was tempered by the Social Gospel. Roddan blamed both the individual and society for the plight of the homeless. The migrant worker was "an indispensable factor in the building of Canada" who nevertheless was cast aside when no longer needed. "We have a form of slavery," he wrote, "which may be worse than the alleged slavery in Russia," an argument that could just as easily have appeared in the *Unemployed Worker*, a communist newspaper of the time, as in the work of a clergyman. Roddan also recognized that the tramping life was not a product of economic need alone but also a form of self-expression on the part of those alienated from society:

> The Bohemian instincts find expression in the life of these men, free to come, free to go, to work or wander, sleep or wake, calling [no] man their master, following th[ei]r own whims and fancies; they want to be free. Perhaps this is a revolt against the kind of life we are all living; where we have bound ourselves by customs, traditions, and habits that hamper life. Maybe the hobo is closer to nature and closer to truth than some of us are. Possessing nothing, he is monarch of all he surveys [....] He is free, the master of his own life, to wander where he likes.

Thus Roddan captured the two-sided character of life in the jungles, recognising the degradations forced on thousands of individuals and their attempt to forge an alternative way of life predicated on both independence and mutuality.

For those on the left, the jungles symbolised not sin but rather the decay of the laissez-faire liberal order. Members of the Independent Labour Party, a forerunner of the Co-operative Commonwealth Federation that was itself the precursor of the New Democratic Party, argued that had the government fulfilled its constitutional responsibilities and cared for the destitute, there would have been no need for people to "live out of doors under conditions that are not fit for human beings." Communists, too, attacked politicians for their obvious failure to provide for those in need. "As this is the busy Tourist season," one communist commentator wrote, "thousands of well fed parasite[s] from the U.S. are able to take in the sight at the city dump, where hundreds of workers are gradually starving to death in the pitiful attempt to salvage an existence from the garbage." Another Bolshevik wag labelled the jungles "samples of Bennett's 'Five Year Plan.'"

Initially Roddan did not dismiss such social critics, particularly since they passionately cared about the homeless. "I only wish the Christian Church could catch something of the missionary zeal which is burning so strong in the heart of the Communist," he wrote. Roddan viewed the issue in light of the "old conflict between economic determinism and spiritual determinism," and he expressed hope that "there must be a *via media* between those two philosophies." But ultimately he returned to the Christian gospel as the true path for the revolutionary, and in this he was not alone. Reverend J.H. White of Sardis, near Chilliwack, expressed the opinion that "the Gospel is the great revolution-ary principle." He went on: "Compared to a disciple of Jesus Christ the red[d]est Communist is only a sickly pink when it comes to fundamental revolution. The Communist will shed the blood of others, the Christian sheds his own."

Roddan's view of the communists grew more conservative; in *The Christ of the Wireless Way,* a collection of his radio talks published in 1932, he included several that established his growing concern with the "materialist" menace, such as "Communism Versus Christianity," "Jesus and the Proletariat," and "Why Stalin Changed His Mind."

Vancouver's jungles were destroyed in early September 1931, following a death attributed to typhoid. Over a thousand men, many from the jungles, were dispatched to labour camps run by the provincial government of Premier Simon Fraser Tolmie, but this measure provided only temporary relief. Jungles would reappear in Vancouver, Kamloops and other spots along the railway lines, and the transient question continued to dominate British Columbia politics. Drawing inspiration from the organising campaign of the Industrial Workers of the World a generation earlier, the Relief Camp Workers' Union conducted more than 100 strikes in government-run relief camps in an attempt to improve the lot of the jobless transient. The Hunger Marches of 1932 and 1933, the mass strike of April 1935 that led to the famous On-to-Ottawa Trek, and the Post Office Sit-In of 1938, all of which were met with considerable police violence, testified to the abiding relevance of the homeless tramp.

Roddan continued to have a measure of political capital throughout the 1930s. While his views of hobo life in the jungles became more conservative over time, he was still one of the few people to strive for a sympathetic understanding of the homeless. First United continued its mission work with the poor of downtown Vancouver, although it ceased its programme in the jungles once the province opened relief camps, whereupon Roddan got caught up in the energy and enthusiasm of the Oxford Movement. He again became a public figure during the 1935 walkout, however, providing aid for striking relief camp residents and for the families of picketing longshoremen. That autumn, he announced over the radio that he endorsed Arnold Webster, candidate for the Co-operative Commonwealth Federation, in his race against Gerald Grattan McGeer for the federal riding of Vancouver-Burrard. McGeer, a foe of the relief-camp strikers, was mayor of Vancouver. And Roddan spoke publicly in support of another leftist cause, the Republican government in Spain, then in the midst of the bloody civil war triggered by a military coup. There are even a few reports that he provided assistance to a number of former On-to-Ottawa trekkers on their way to fight in Spain as part of the Mackenzie-Papineau Battalion. Roddan also continued to produce books and pamphlets to further his causes. Most contain more than one reference to the jungle mission that had so captivated public attention in 1931. Perhaps a hint of pride showed through. Roddan served at First United until his death in April 1948.

Todd McCallum
Dalhousie University

# TO MY HOMELESS BROTHERS

The foxes have holes, and the birds of the air have nests;
but the Son of Man hath not where to lay His head.

*Matthew 8:20*

## The "Drifter" Speaks

I'm the man you call a drifter,
Chased by cops from town to town;
I can carry in my 'kerchief
All the real estate I own.

In my quest for bread and butter
I have travelled near and far;
Many times I've asked this question:
"Say, old top, who won the war?"

Some would say the Yankees won it,
Others say 'twas British pluck.
That makes me the guy who lost it
And my health in Flanders muck.

That's the reason no one needs me;
Those who slapped me on the back,
Cheered me when I fought for freedom,
Jeered me when I drifted back.

P.S.—I'm not a Red, my well-fed brother;
Though I drift to hell and back,
I can still sing "Rule Britannia"
And salute the Union Jack.

Author unknown
(veteran of two wars, no fixed abode).
From the *Vancouver Sun.*

# God in the Jungles

Remember, my friend, whoever you may be, when you read this story, that is not a study of the complicated problem of unemployment nor a compilation of statistics dealing with facts and figures in the abstract. It is a story of human interest dealing with flesh and blood, telling you in a simple and direct manner something of the struggle for an existence on the part of thousands of homeless men in this great Canada of ours.

As superintendent of First United Church, Vancouver, Canada, "the Church of the Open Door," I have had a unique opportunity of meeting these men personally and dealing with them in a very direct and practical manner. They have come to First Church for food, shelter, clothing, shoes, as well as counsel and spiritual help through the church services on Sunday.

The great majority of these homeless men want work; there is absolutely no doubt about that in my mind. During the winter of 1930 and 1931 and right on until the end of August, we gave food to over 50,000 men. Our bread line at its highest was 1,252 men long in one day. We recognize the fact that this is not a solution of the problem, but when every other door was practically closed we opened up and gave food to the men. While the politicians, councillors and businessmen were holding conferences and talk-fests we were giving the men food every day. Our vans have gone down to the jungles in the different parts of this district every day, and distributed food to the men.

On Christmas day we provided, in conjunction with other United churches in Vancouver, a Christmas dinner for 250 men. As we had many different nationalities represented, the minister of the Russian Church, which holds its services in First United, spoke to the Russians, and brought them a Christmas greeting. The Finnish minister whose congregation also meets in the church brought greetings to the Finns. Our Scandinavian minister brought Christmas greetings to all Scandinavians and then I talked to the others, and brought a message of hope and encouragement to these homeless men on Christmas Day.

This, then, is the purpose of the book: to create a sympathetic understanding of the life and problems of the homeless men.

It is estimated there are over 50,000 in Canada of all nationalities, creeds and conditions, from the university graduate to the most illiterate and ignorant type of men.

In the name of the Master, who Himself in a sense was a homeless man, and who knew what it was to experience that sense of utter loneliness when he said, "The foxes have holes and the birds of the air have nests, but the Son of Man has not where to lay His head." We remember that He also said, "The Son of Man has come to seek and to save that which is lost," and so we who profess His Name can do no less than hear His call and lend a hand to these homeless men.

## ⋆ THE JUNGLES ⋆

When you think of a jungle you imagine a dense tropical forest with heavy, tangled undergrowth, where the light of the sun rarely penetrates and which is the haunt of wild beasts and savage men. The jungles of which I write and the ones which I describe in particular present a very different picture before the mind.

They may be found in clumps of wild bushes or among the trees, on the side of a stream, by the side of the road, near the railroad tracks, or in a disused lumber camp or factory. They are to be found in Australia, India, Japan and in Great Britain as well as in Canada and America.

Look at the picture and you will see that this jungle is composed of crude shelters made out of old tins, boards, boxes, disused motorcars, anything and everything, gathered from the dump heap nearby and formed into a rough shelter into which crawl, not animals, but homeless men, without saying their prayers, feeling as the Psalmist felt when he said: "No man careth for my soul." Their bellies slack and gnawing with hunger, they lie down and go to sleep, while the other half sleep in hotels and comfortable homes. In the jungles they look up at the stars, and the rats are the only animals to be found there.

From Toronto and Halifax across Canada to Vancouver, along the main lines of traffic close by every city and village they are to be found. It may be only a temporary place sheltering two or four, or it may attain considerable proportions like those of which I have made a closer study. The people may not be aware of its presence, but it is known to every hobo who is riding the rods, as the word is passed along. The jungle is to the hobo what the auto camp is to the tourist. A place where he can rest up and prepare for the next day.

I shall not forget the impressions that were registered on my mind on my first visit to the jungles right in my own parish in the city of Vancouver. There was a mental and moral revolt that made my heart feel sick that it could be possible in this young country of Canada to have a situation like this. I felt like crying out to high Heaven against this condition, and I will continue to do so until church and state recognize their mutual responsibility towards these thousands of homeless men.

When the Honourable Gideon Robertson, the minister of Labour, visited Vancouver I told him in an interview that when I stood in the jungles and saw the conditions there I did not know whether I was in Russia or in Canada. I told him I had just finished reading the book by Sherwood Eddy, entitled *The Challenge of Russia*, and I had not seen any picture or read any story that equalled that condition as a breeding place for Bolshevism. The only difference was this: that in Russia they would be put to work, while in Canada we allowed strong men such as you see to deteriorate in idleness through no fault of their own.

A jungle is oftentimes a miniature League of Nations. As I walked through among the men and talked to them I found there were many nationalities and many languages spoken. Strangely enough the first man I spoke to was a Scotsman from Aberdeen, "Awa": "This is the first time I have been in a place like this," he said, with a sense of shame. "When I came to Canada I never thought I would get so low down. I would be ashamed to have my people know where I am today." Another from Forfar. You should have seen him smile when I mentioned Forfar Bridies.

Here is another picture of a Scotsman. I am not telling him a fish story, but making some remark about the dimensions of the shack he is building and the following is a copy of a letter from his dear old mother:

My Dear James:

I was fair upset when Maggie came to me with your letter, for I thought you were lost; but, no, Jim, you can just think of me alone now, but I aye had a idea you would write sometime, but what a blow I got when I read Bob's death in the evening paper. It was more than I could think it was true till I made enquiries to Aberdeen. However, Jim, he has left a weary world of toil and pain. There is nothing but troubles and disappointment here below. We will, I trust, all meet again up Yonder where all is peace and joy.

Now I hope you are trying to do your best and that you get that pension you speak of.

I am well pleased to be able to get that paper for you and hope you succeed now. I am a poor lonely old woman, 77 years old. Jim, I never thought to live such a time, but God's time is worth waiting for, and I wait patiently.

Now Maggie is in the furnace just now. Her little boy Andrew is in the Hospital this eight weeks, but he is getting on. He may get home for the Christmas, but will have to go back for a wee while. Now, Jim, I do not know what more to say, but I am to put this in with Maggie's box, hoping you get it all safe. With best love and wishes, from your old and lonely

Mother.

Walking over to another group, I found them to be Finns; great, strong, husky men. Now the Finn is instinctively clean in his habits and person, and even here in the jungle amid this environment, I found them keeping themselves clean.

These men were brought out to Canada to work in the big industries, to work in lumber camps, mines, railroad construction work. As I looked at these men I could see some of them were the type of man I had seen in the lumber camps of British

Columbia. Men with grit and ability thinking nothing of climbing a tree 250 feet, cutting off the top, standing on it and rolling a cigarette, and here they were wasting their lives in idleness through no fault of their own.

Another group were Germans, great, big strong men living together with a group of Norwegians and Scandinavians. Some of the finest types of men we have in the Dominion of Canada. While right in the centre of the bush I found a miniature Chinatown.

There is a spirit of comradeship. I can understand now what Robert Burns meant when he said: "A fellow-feeling makes us wondrous kind." There is a common brotherhood forced, no doubt, by stern necessity. It is that kind of brotherhood we find when the forest fire sweeps the mountainside and animals and human beings flee together from a common foe. Here, then, is the place where these men can seek a refuge and share what they have.

We organized the work and got the men to assist in the distribution of food, and in all the serving of thousands of men I have yet to hear the first angry word or the first swear word from anyone of the men. When one old chap was not able to fix his shack some of the stronger men got together and built him a place to crawl in and go to sleep.

When a man comes into the jungles after having been on the train for a week or two weeks, you would not know whether he was white or black. Dust begrimed he comes in, no questions are asked. He hunts around for a place for himself and tells of his experiences. Anything of his past life is given voluntarily and so long as he plays the game he is allowed to stay.

I saw to it that the men had plenty of fresh water in the jungle. They are domesticated through years of practice. These men have been accustomed to this kind of life and others are being initiated every day. It is a marvel with their limited resources and conveniences that they are able to keep their camp clean, wash their clothes, do their sewing, without the help of a woman.

# ✦ THE MAN WITHOUT A HOME ✦

When you visit a jungle such as I have described, or look on a long line of men waiting for food in a bread line or you see them standing in groups outside the employment office in the city; or when they climb your porch or accost you on the street for a hand-out, if you are a thinking man or woman you wonder who they are, why they are here, where they come from and what will their future be?

When a man on the street meets a panhandler he usually gets rid of him by giving him a coin. The authorities put him in jail as a vagrant. To the social worker he is a problem, a case to be studied; the cause of his condition to be investigated and a remedy to be found. We must attack this whole problem in a scientific, Christian spirit and not allow sentimentality to slop over and obscure the facts.

The homeless men in Canada have become one of the major social problems, particularly in our Coast cities and centres of population. Generally speaking these men may be divided into groups or classes. St. John Tucker, formerly president of the Hobo College in Chicago, has classed them as follows: "A hobo is a migratory worker," "A tramp is a migratory non-worker," "A bum is a stationary non-worker"; or they have been further defined by Ben L. Reitman, who has been called the King of the Hoboes, who says there are three types of genus vagrant: "The hobo, the tramp, the bum." The hobo works and wanders, the tramp dreams and wanders, the bum drinks and wanders. Then added to this list there is the Homeguard, who, like the poor, are always with us.

# ✦ THE HOBO ✦

The hobo is a migratory worker, a man who travels about from place to place looking for work. When a notice is posted in the

21

Employment Office that some construction work is about to start, this man and his class make for the location as soon as possible. They still have something of the spirit of independence left in them, and they are anxious to make enough money to get by on the next winter. They form the regular hobo class, workers in disposition and wanderers by compulsion.

The hobo has been described in the following lines from *John O' London's Weekly*, which sum up the kind of life he leads in a graphic way:

A hobo is a man who builds palaces and lives in shacks,
He builds Pullmans and rides the rods,
He builds automobiles and pushes a wheelbarrow,
He serves T-bone steaks and gets the soup bone,
He builds electric-light plants and burns oil,
He builds opera houses and goes to the movies,
He makes silk suspenders and holds his pants up with a rope,
He reaps the harvest and stands in the bread line,
He weaves silk shirts and wears bull wool,
He makes broadcloth and wears overalls,
He weaves linen sheets and sleeps on a plank,
He digs gold and has his teeth filled with cement,
He digs coal and shivers in the snow,
He builds the factories and is denied a job in them,
He builds skyscrapers and has no place to call a home,
He builds roads and is arrested on them for vagrancy,
He creates labour and is denied the right to labour,
He fights for freedom abroad and is put on the chain gang at home,
He has made Canada and is denied a vote.

I take my hat off to the hobo. He has been an indispensable factor in the building of Canada. Without his strong muscles the railways, canals, bridges, tunnels, and public works of many kinds could never have been carried out. While we think of the architect and the engineer, with their brains and blueprints, let us not forget the man who, with his pick and shovel, helped to make their plans a reality. They are the men who have developed our natural resources. The pioneers in the opening of new lands and the construction of great private and public works.

As a rule they are a good class of men, rough and uncouth on the outside, but when you come to know them they are very human, generous, and responsive to a touch of kindness, especially when they know there is nothing of cant or insincerity about it. The irregularity of their work has a very serious reaction on their outlook on society and life in general. The lack of permanence tends to demoralize the man and while in the vigour of his manhood he is able to stand the racket, the advance of years begins to tell on him and he goes down physically, socially, and morally until he finds himself in the ranks of the homeguard, at the bottom of the list.

Under our present system 1,000 or 5,000 of this class of men may be employed on some public work or private enterprise. When the work is done and with due pomp and ceremony the wheels of industry are set in motion and the skilled workers stand by the machine, the hoboes are soon forgotten and they vanish away. They know there is no further use for them in that locality and they put themselves in the "Slave Market," as they call it and, like the man in the parable, wait for someone to hire them.

### The Slave Market

This is the city of lost dreams and defeated hopes;
Always you are the Mecca of the Jobless,
The seekers after life and the sweet illusions of happiness.
Within your walls there are the consuming
Fires of pain, sorrow and eternal regrets.
Roses never bloom here; silken petals

Cannot be defiled.
Streets in ragged attire, sang-froid in their violence;
Years come and go; still your hideousness goes on
And mute outcasts garnish
Your every rendezvous.
Blind pigs, reeking with a nauseous smell everywhere;
The so-called "flops," the lousy beds
Where slaves of mill and mine and rail and shop
Curl up and drop away unconscious
In fair pretence of sleep.
Employment sharks entrapping men,
Human vultures in benign disguise,
Auctioning labour at a pittance per day.
And it's always, "What will you give?"
"What will you take?"
The pocketing of fat commissions;
Old men, young men, tramps, bums, hoboes,
Labourers seeking jobs or charity
Each visioning happiness from afar.

They swarm the city streets, these slaves,
For all must live and strive,
And always the elusive job sign
Greets their contemplative glance,
A job—food, clothing, shelter;
Wage slaves selling their power;
Oh, you Slave Market, I know you!

From timbered lands, North, East, South and West,
From distant golden grain belts,
From endless miles of rail,
These workers float to the city.
Timber beasts, harvesters, gandy dancers,
Adventurers all. From every clime and zone,

Each comes with hope of work or
Else to blow his pile.

(With acknowledgement to Louis Melis,
well-known poet of hobo life.)

They may be fortunate to strike it with some company with a sense of justice and honour in their dealings with these men or they may be at the mercy of some unscrupulous contractor or concern, where no fair-wage clause has been inserted in the contract, and we have a form of slavery which may be worse than the alleged slavery in Russia. The fault is not all his for the condition in which he finds himself; society must take its share of the blame.

I gratefully acknowledge the help received from the reading of the book entitled *The Hobo*, by Prof. Nels Anderson.

## ✦ THE TRAMP ✦

The tramp is the man who has the wanderlust in his nature, but who will not work if he can get by. To the casual observer it might be hard to distinguish the difference between a tramp and a hobo, but if you have been dealing with this class of men you instinctively sum a man up by his conversation, the answers he will give you to your questions, where he has been working, his hesitancy to register at the Government Employment Office or carry a card, the general appearance of his clothes. However, I have found that it is always better to give a man the benefit of the doubt. I have been fooled many times, but there have been other occasions when I would have done a man great injury by a premature judgment of his case.

The tramp has no purpose in his life. If he hears of any public works opening up he determines he will not be there. They are experts at begging, resorting to all manner of tricks, and with ready tongue they find it is easier than work, and settle down to that kind of life. For a time they will stay and work a town or district and then move on aimlessly like derelicts on the ocean of life.

## ⚊ THE BUM ⚊

This class corresponds to the homeguard and moocher. The bum is a stationary non-worker. Many of them were first a problem in the home and at school and then to society in general. I have stood with them on the scaffold and seen them ushered two at a time into Eternity. I have met them as murderers who have done long terms in prison. Here, in this class, you will find the drug addicts, coke-eaters, alcoholics, moral perverts, morons, feeble-minded, canned-heat artists, and if there be any other class or type of depraved humanity, you can put them in this category. When day after day as the bread line passes by, you learn to pick them out by their bleary eyes, shaky hands, trembling bodies, unkempt appearance, dirty clothes, gabbling tongues, always grousing about something or somebody, or sullen, morose and quiet.

In this class we find ourselves face to face with the human derelict. The ocean is strewn with them, like the derelicts of the sea, some of them are rudderless and water-logged. Some of them turned turtle and become a menace to all who cross their paths. When I meet this type of homeless man it always recalls to my mind an incident when I was in service on the Rock of Gibraltar. The *Assistance*, repair ship to the Atlantic squadron, had gone out with the fleet to Tetuan, off the coast of Africa, to stand by while they were doing heavy gun practice. During the night she dragged anchor and went on the rocks. They thought all was well, but did not realize the danger, until she grounded on the rocky shore, and then it was too late. It cost the British

Government a large amount of money to salvage the ship.

The human derelict is a problem wherever you may meet him and in the long run, a costly member of society. In this group I have found university graduates; one man I knew, a graduate of Glasgow University, could quote Greek and Latin by the page. College men from good homes. One man, a great big fellow, to whom I had to look up, and I am six feet, told me he had two brothers, both ministers, in Scotland. He gave me their names and particulars, but he was ashamed to write and let them know of his condition. He would rather die. His people had given him up as dead. Another whose father was a Wesleyan-Methodist minister and who had received a good education, came to me one day. He had taken the wrong turn, evil habits had conquered him and he had lost out in the fight. Another man with whom I dealt in the condemned cell before he was hanged had not written home for 25 years. When I wrote to his people they received a terrible shock, as they thought he was dead, and when they knew the circumstances they wished they had never known the awful truth. He was hanged under an assumed name.

Another young man in whom I was interested had finished a long term of imprisonment in the penitentiary. I intervened on his behalf and he was released. The story got into the newspapers and a man came all the way from Toronto to see me, enquiring if this was his nephew, in whom he was interested, and who was now heir to a large estate. I shall never forget the look of disappointment on his countenance when I informed him, after getting the particulars, that this was not the same man.

In this class you will find men with an aristocratic type of face: remittance men who have been sent out from the Old Country because of their disgraceful habits, to save the family name. Their main means of support seems to be blackmailing their people in the Old Country with the threat that they will turn up some day and disgrace the family unless some money is forthcoming. This threat usually has effect until they kill themselves with their excesses and I am called in to bury them.

The bum is so low that the regular hoboes in the jungles will have nothing to do with them. They are at the bottom of the scale, some of them lower than the beasts of the fields.

A man stumbled into the church the other day, a regular dead-beat, one of the lowest types possible. He was a cripple with a crutch. He had been falling on the pavement, his face was battered and bleeding–what a sight–ugly and repulsive. My first impulse was to bawl him out, and then looking at him I remembered the words of the Master, "I came not to call the righteous but sinners to repentance, the Son of Man has come to seek and to save that which was lost." I asked myself, "Does God love the hobo, the tramp, the bum, the moocher? Does God love this poor wretch in front of me?" The answer came, "Yes. While He hates the sin, He loves the sinner."

I am one of those who believe that a man may be down but he is never out until, conquered by his evil habits, he takes the count against himself and the Devil wins.

## ✦ WHY MEN LEAVE HOME ✦

Having in some measure attempted to explain who these men are and some of their modes of "getting by," as they express it in hobo land, the next question which naturally arises is how do they become floaters and drifters, and what are the reasons why they failed to make good; what are the factors which entered into their lives preventing them from becoming useful citizens. I have asked many of these men these questions and every man seems to have a different excuse, explanation or reason to give for his present predicament. It is best not to accept their story without taking all the factors into consideration, as self-diagnosis is always a dangerous procedure in any case. After having passed through the hard school of experience, in which most fools learn something, many of them are ready to admit that the main trouble has not been with society, but with themselves, and looking back they can see where they might have taken a different course.

This does not apply to all cases, however, and we shall now give our attention to a study of some of the factors which have entered into their lives and made them negative and practically useless.

Many of the men with whom I have talked started out on the journey of life with the best of intentions, and then something went wrong; some disappointment came to them–bad luck, as they call it, pursued them–ill-health and serious physical handicaps deterred them; domestic trouble, personal problems, lack of ambition and aggressiveness–all these and many others might be given.

## WANDERLUST

Through experience I have learned that some men are born with this spirit of wandering in their nature. It is a difficult thing to define, but it certainly has played an important part in the development of human society. Early in the history of the human race, sometimes by force of necessity in the search for food, and freedom, there have been great migrations of population and that spirit seems to have been inherited by many individuals since the time that Abraham responded to that inner urge that led him to leave his Father's home, as we read in Genesis 12 and 1: "Get thee out of thy country and from thy kindred and from thy Father's land into the land which I shall show thee." Since that time and long before, man has been a wanderer on the face of the earth.

One of the main differences between the new land and the old is that here in Canada it is largely a problem of the single homeless men, whereas in the Old Country it is a problem of the family, mixed groups of women and children, but now a change is taking place and increasing numbers of women are joining "the Knights of the Rods," and they are learning to live in jungles like the men.

In Great Britain and Europe these wanderers are known as gypsies and the caravans and wagons, with their basketware, are well known to those of the Old Lands.

Then we have the tinkers, tramps, cadgers, constantly on the move, drifting hither and thither, living in jungles in the summer and cheap lodging houses in the winter. The spirit of wandering has taken men and women far afield. In some degree it accounts for our expansion as a nation and as an empire. The pioneers of Great Britain had it in their blood, the explorers and adventurers like Raleigh, Cook, Drake, Vancouver, Mackenzie, Fraser, to mention only a few, were animated by that spirit. Sometimes it was stern necessity, as in the case of the Pilgrim Fathers and the Selkirk settlers, that led them to the shores of Canada to explore its rivers, lakes, mountains. Some stayed in the East, others passed on to the West, now they are pressing towards the North. The main difference, of course, is obvious to all: those pioneer explorers had a definite plan and destination—the hobo has none.

### ⁕ THE HOBO AN INDIVIDUALIST ⁕

Many of these homeless men have been born that way. They are individualists, they refuse to submit to discipline, or training of any kind. In the home, the school or the community they are a problem and our present system is not able to deal with them.

The Bohemian instincts find expression in the life of these men, free to come, free to go, to work or wander, sleep or wake, calling on man their master, following their own whims and fancies; they want to be free. Perhaps this is a revolt against the kind of life we are all living; where we have bound ourselves by customs, traditions, and habits that hamper life. Maybe the hobo is closer to nature and closer to truth than some of us are. Possessing nothing, he is monarch of all he surveys. A stock crash does not matter to him so long as he can collect enough for the mulligan pot; special railway rates and timetables do not interest him because he can hit the trail when he feels like it and walk or ride or catch the freight on the fly for nowhere in particular, just as the spirit moves him. The changing fashions amuse the hobo. A shirt, a pair of overalls, socks and boots are all he has to worry about. He is free, the master of his own life, to wander where he likes.

## ⚹ THE JUVENILE HOBO ⚹

In Canada we are face to face with a new phase of this problem which presents a real challenge, to church and society. I have been astonished to find many boys in their early teens standing in the bread line. Here is a young lad just turned sixteen, who came all the way from Montreal. It took him three weeks to travel to Vancouver. During that time he had met and mixed with some of the roughest and toughest types of men in the Dominion of Canada.

He had no home, his parents had both died and he was left to take care of himself and so, being a free lance, he set out to see Vancouver. He landed in Vancouver without food or shelter. Hearing about First Church, he came to our door and we were able to help him.

Another lad of sixteen, just out of high school in Toronto, came to us one day in our bread line. I took him aside and asked him why he was here. He told me that he could get no work and he had heard that in Vancouver there was a better chance. He told his father and mother he did not want to be a burden on them, so he jumped the freight for the Coast.

While stationed in the city of Port Arthur, Ontario, two young fellows came to my door one evening asking for help. I enquired where they had come from, and they told me, "From Montreal." "And where are you going?" I asked. They said, "To Vancouver." I said, "Why?" Because they had heard work was better and it was easier to live in Vancouver.

After they had done some work for me, for which I paid them, they left. They had scarcely gone when two other young fellows came along and I put the same questions to them: Where had they come from? "From Vancouver." Where were they heading for? "Toronto." And why Toronto? Because they had heard they were opening up work in Toronto. And that is the typical experience of thousands of these men who are wandering to and fro across the Dominion of Canada.

Another young man from Coalmont, Alberta, came to the church with much the same story. He wanted to go back home again, and we fixed him up with clothes and food, and the CPR gave him a free ride on the 10:10 from Vancouver. We received a grateful letter from him saying that after a hard experience he had got home.

Whenever we have found boys in the bread line, I have made a special appeal to the farmers in the Fraser Valley over the radio, over CKFC, the radio station of the United Church of Canada. We speak to an audience of 50,000 every Sunday morning. This special appeal has never failed to bring a response from some of the farmers, and we have been able to place many of them in good homes.

The Honourable Senator [Gideon] Robertson told us during the interview we had in Vancouver, that at one point in Ontario three high school boys had boarded the train, one of whom was the son of a personal friend of his. Another young lad, who had won the Governor-General's Medal in high school, was found in the camp.

With many of these boys the problem is psychological: the desire to travel and see Canada first and free. These cases are the exception and not the rule. Great numbers of these young lads have got sick and tired of hunting jobs that were not there and of being a burden on their parents. They beat it on the train for other parts.

One of our own ministers told me of his experience in his home with his own boys. When they found it impossible to get employment they threatened to board the train and get out of the city, where they had been born, raised and educated because no man would hire them and they could not apply for relief, and so were a burden on their parents. "Dad," they said, "if we go to Calgary or Edmonton they will feed us anyway, which is more than we can get here." Good counsel prevailed, however, but that father had a real problem on his hands.

There are thousands of teenaged youths riding the rods. Ask the policemen and the trainmen and those in our social centres across Canada and they will verify this statement.

The horror of it all is that these boys are being inoculated with wrong ideas through their contact with all kinds of men in freight cars, in jungles, across Canada.

It cost the state a large amount of money to educate them. They have brought untold grief to the hearts of anxious parents. They represent a social, moral and economic loss, to the whole community, and it is high time something was being done about it to prevent them from developing into hoboes, tramps, and bums.

## ⁕ THE PRODIGAL HOBO ⁕

His case can be summed up under the following headings: Sick of home, Homesick, Home. There are still those young men who, like the younger son in the parable, get fed up with home life, grow discontented with conditions and things in general. They kick over the traces, there is a racket and they demand what is coming to them, then beat it as quick as they can and as far as they can go from home. It is the old story—as long as their money lasts they have a good time and plenty of friends in the far country.

When they come to themselves they are homesick and some of the wiser ones go home and admit to Dad that they were not as wise as they thought they were, and home looks pretty good after their experience, and they stay there. But, friends, I am stating the truth when I say that thousands of these boys never go back, and to all intents and purposes they are lost, wandering boys on the face of the earth.

They change their name, and sin and evil living does the rest, so that even their own flesh and blood would scarcely recognize them when the years have passed.

We need a new emphasis on that word *lost*, and the church and state need to be awakened to a sense of its responsibility to these wandering sons of Adam.

## ✦ THE MISFITS ✦

There are those men who don't fit in. Their case is well stated by Robert W. Service, the well-known poet of the Yukon, in his book *The Spirit of the Yukon*.

### *The Men That Don't Fit In*

There's a race of men that don't fit in,
A race that can't stay still;
So they break the hearts of kith and kin,
And roam the world at will.
They range the field and they rove the flood,

And they climb the mountain crest;
Theirs is the curse of the gypsy blood,
And they don't know how to rest.

If they just went straight they might go far;
They are strong and brave and true;
But they're always tired of the things that are,
And they want the strange and new.
They say: "Could I find my proper groove,
What a deep mark I would make!"
So they chop and change, and each fresh move
Is only a fresh mistake.

And each forgets as he strips and runs
With a brilliant, fitful pace,
It's the steady, quiet, plodding ones
Who win the lifelong race.
And each forgets that his youth has fled,
Forgets that his prime is past,
Till he stand one day with a hope that's dead,
In the glare of the truth at last.

The ancient Hebrews made it a rule that every boy must learn to use his hands as well as his head. It was no accident that the Apostle Paul was a tent-maker, the high priest a baker, and Jesus a carpenter; it was all part of a well-thought plan that everyone should have a trade, and by exercising his knowledge and skill with his hands and head he would be able to take care of himself and maintain his independence.

In the days of the Guilds in Europe and Britain, every boy learned a trade in the village or community where he was born, and there were fewer misfits, comparatively speaking, than under our present system. The blacksmith, the harness-maker, the baker, the tailor, the mason, and the various other tradesmen had their apprentices working with them. Usually a boy followed his father's vocation and all fitted in to some niche.

It seems to me in spite of our technical and vocational systems of education we are still in quite a muddle in dealing with this problem. Think, for example, of the thousands of boys who are being sent out to this country from institutions in the Old Country, and the only object in bringing them out was to put them on to a farm and make them farmers when God had intended some of them to be mechanics, artists, and leaders in industry.

There is something radically wrong in a system that turns out thousands of graduates from our educational institutions, fitted with costly equipment, highly paid, well-trained teachers, and no jobs and no work for these boys to do. There are yet many gaps to be filled and because we have not fully dealt with the situation there are still many misfits.

In the early pioneer days of Canada the population was largely self-supporting. Their needs and wants were simple. The bear, the buffalo, the sheep, provided them with food and clothing to keep them warm. The forest produced all they required to build their homes, make their furniture and fuel for the winter fire. The rivers and lakes filled with fish and the earth brought forth abundant harvest. The herbs, roots and barks kept them supplied with nature's medicine and thus in a practical way their needs were met.

The wanderer was always welcome in the lonely pioneer places. He brought the news from the outside world and, as [the popular nature writer and journalist] Uncle Jack Miner expresses it, they learn to live on three meals a day–"oatmeal, cornmeal and miss-a-meal." Men did not wander far afield before they found a place in life. Now it is impossible, as we have become so dependent on other people and other nations to supply us with the necessaries of life. Therefore, because thousands of these young men when they graduate from school do not find a place in life and nobody particularly cares whether they do or not, they are left to shift for themselves, the door of opportunity is closed, and they begin to drift and go down.

Another phase of this problem has been the result of the policy of the government in the year 1927 when they brought over thousands of miners from the Old Country to go into the harvest fields. Large numbers of these men went back home again, but several thousand remained. I have met and talked with many of these men, and I am convinced that a great mistake was made and that large numbers of these men are becoming bums and tramps because there was no individual to follow them up and now many of them are lined up with the homeguard.

They will be a social problem in every community where they may be found because they have failed to fit into Canadian lives and ways, and because the state took no interest in them after the harvest was reaped.

## ⚘ WHY MEN FAIL ⚘

Few men are willing to admit that they are failures. Of those who are ready to face the fact, a large number will persist in wondering "Why?" Few will ever blame themselves.

Why do we fail? The Life Insurance Sales Research Bureau gives a rather interesting table of reasons under which the palpable failure may hide his diminished head.

Out of 100 men: 37 fail for lack of industry, 37 fail because discouraged, 12 fail by not following instructions, eight fail for lack of knowledge, four fail through dishonesty, two fail because of ill-luck.

There are, of course, other reasons that could be listed, but the above are fairly comprehensive. It is noticeable that a goodly percentage fail for lack of industry. The man who won't work cannot expect to get very far. In an age of keen competition it is only the industrious who can hold their own with any measure of success. The lazy man is doomed to failure from the outset. And how many will admit they are lazy?

An equal number lapse because of discouragement. It is very easy to become dispirited, to feel that all the world is against you. But when a man begins to feel sorry for himself, he begins at the same moment to lose his grip.

It is frequently hard to combat discouragement, but the fellow who is sufficiently optimistic to look beyond an unhappy present with faith in future opportunities is not predestined to failure.

Twelve out of a hundred fail by not following instructions. There are and always will be men and women who know it all. They can't be told anything. Their way is best. They disregard instructions from those who are in a position to guide their steps and if they fail—as statistics show they do—they naturally blame someone else. Their own pig-headedness is not taken into consideration.

Eight percent fail from lack of knowledge. Herein the failure may not be entirely to blame. The foundation of his education or his apprenticeship may have been lacking. His ignorance may be due to forces beyond his control. At the same time, a man who does not know his job is but a square peg in a round hole. He is a misfit, doomed to failure from the outset.

Only four percent fail through dishonesty. The dishonest worker is a failure from an ethical viewpoint no matter where he is placed. Inevitably his sin will find him out. The liar, the cheat, or the thief is bound to come a cropper, sooner or later. He has no place in the general scheme of things. Whether he juggles in high finance or indulges in dishonest acts on a small scale, he does not belong among honest people.

## ⚊ THE WHITE COLLAR BRIGADE ⚊

It is a common thing to find in the bread line men who have been accustomed to clerical work and who find themselves there, through no fault of their own, the victims of circumstances over which they have no control. The introduction of office machinery—adding, subtracting and checking machines—has eliminated the bookkeeper and the accountant and now they are standing in the bread line and for the first time in their lives they know not which way to turn. They are not fit to work in the relief gang, digging ditches. Some of them have gone out and broken down, taken sick, died, and I have buried them. They have become a burden on the state, not able to adjust themselves to new conditions.

## ⚊ BOOM DAYS ⚊

Large numbers of these men were persuaded to leave their homes in the Old Country and come to Canada. The shipping agents, the railway companies and contractors brought these men out by the thousand for construction work of all kinds. They were needed to do what the machine could not and never can do. There was no limit to the number brought to Canada. Indeed, it was thought in some quarters that there was a deliberate attempt to bring in large numbers of these men so as to flood the labour market and keep wages down. I do not know how far that was true, but one thing is certain, that the heartless manner in which these men have been dumped on the labour market when the work has been completed and the indifference to their spiritual and moral needs leaves the impression on their minds that nobody cares for them when they are down and out. They are the product of a badly organized social, religious and economic system.

Andrew Roddan

## ~ THE HOBO AND THE CLIMATE ~

It is a well known fact that thousands of these homeless men flock to the Coast cities of Canada for the winter months. They know they will not freeze on the Coast and there will always be a chance on the "Stem" of "gettin' by" somehow.

During normal times these men make enough money in the lumber camp, in the cannery, in the mines, on the boats and in the harvest fields to get by during the winter. When they have a roll of two hundred or three hundred dollars, everybody gives them the glad hand because they have a little money.

The owners of cheap lodging houses give them board and room while their money lasts. Although I must say some of them during this past winter have been very considerate to these men by giving them credit, trusting that when they get work they will make good and pay their debt.

During a time of depression so universal as that of the present year, thousands of these men found it impossible to get by, and for the first time in their lives they had to depend on others for help.

It was pitiful to listen to some of their stories as they told of having sold all they had to keep body and soul together, until at last they were down to what they had on their back.

Then there are personal factors. When you look into the faces of some of these homeless men you realize that they are defective personalities and of a subnormal type. There is a spirit of instability manifest among them. They have not been able to match up to the demands of modern life. There is evidence of emotional instability. Many of them learned their first lesson by playing truant from school. They were not able to make the grade and developed a dislike of anything that required mental effort. They rebelled against discipline. They lacked the power of concentration and these things have placed a serious handicap on their lives. Many of these men never knew what a home was; they had no happiness in their childhood. Many of them never experienced the love of a father or mother. They had been left to the mercy of the world, or if placed in institutions they resented the discipline. When talking to some of these men, one realizes the value of a good home, and the powerful influence of environment on human life and experience.

Sometimes an act of indiscretion and a sense of shame has cost many a young man to overestimate the wrong done and he has disappeared from the community. For years he may wander on the face of the earth, and the longer he is away, because of his egocentricity, the more he magnifies this problem.

Even as I write this, a young man has come to my office from the penitentiary where he served five years, and now he feels he cannot go back to his friends. He prefers to quit the old home rather than face the criticism of the community.

## ⚹ THE BOSS ⚹

There are some employers and foremen who have not lost that fellow-feeling that makes the whole world kin. There are others who have just enough brains to keep them above the brute level, but who are as coarse as animals in their attitude to those who happen to be under their control. They have the bullying nature in them, and their main qualifications seem to be a stentorian voice, a temper as hot as Hades and a vocabulary that includes every swear word ever invented or conceived by the depraved mind of man.

The following actual incident illustrates what I mean: a foreman was watching a foreigner doing a job. Suddenly, because of a slip the man made, the foreman burst forth into a terrible tirade of abuse. "Here you d— bohunk, what the h— are you doing?" The man turned for a moment, surprised at hearing the word *bohunk*, and he replied "Me no bohunk, me Canadian; me drink, me smoke, me swear—me Canadian," and according to his idea of a Canadian he was ready to fight the boss to a finish. After a while that kind of treatment destroys a man's respect, and he quits and moves on to another camp to get a worse dose than before.

## ⁜ THE MACHINE AGE ⁜

One of the main factors in the disorganization of labour in this age is the modern machine. Each year thousands of human hands are being displaced through the introduction of machinery. I can remember when I was a boy the old-fashioned hand looms, slow but sure. Then I can remember the introduction of the fast power loom with the shuttle moving at lightning speed, with one man or woman tending several machines. Thousands of miners will never again go beneath the surface to follow the vocation for which they have been trained, because of the introduction of oil burners in ships and railroad engines, the development of electric power, and the harnessing of millions of white horses; the modern use of white fuel instead of black, for cooking and heating, has changed the outlook of the whole mining industry.

The construction of powerful locomotives capable of hauling trains a mile long has meant displacement of train crews representing thousands of men.

When a great building is to be erected and the excavation is started, previously a small army of men with teams of horses, shovels and wheelbarrows did the work. Now only a few men are required and a great, black throbbing monster rips and tears the earth, lifts it by the ton, as a mother would her baby, deposits it in powerful caterpillar trucks that can drag themselves out of the deep holes in the excavation.

The other day one of the large companies located in one of the big cities of Canada advertised for five hundred men; fifteen hundred swarmed the employment office seeking for work. When they saw those huge machines they became enraged and tried to destroy them, just as a hundred years ago they attacked the loom and spinning machines in England.

The same changes are taking place in the farm. It is not many years since the farmers required a great army of men to help with the harvest. Now, with the introduction of machinery, and particularly the combine, the average farmer is able to handle the crop with only a very few hands.

Not many years ago, at the head of the Lakes, where I resided for a time, all the grain was loaded by wheelbarrows and hundreds of men were kept busy pouring it into the holds of the freighters. Now a modern ship like the *Lemoyne* can load 560,000 bushels of grain in less than four hours. It is not necessary to elaborate on this point. We are living in the machine age. It is working in every part of industry. It has come to stay, and we have not yet been able to adjust ourselves to new conditions. Thousands of men each year are being set adrift because of the introduction of machinery.

This story in the *Province* will help to illustrate more clearly what I have in mind:

## ✵ A TALE OF A POLE ✵

There was an excellent object lesson, outside the office of the *Province* yesterday, in that condition which has come to be known as technological unemployment. To give more room for traffic on Cambie Street, the sidewalk along Victory Square is to be narrowed, and it has become necessary to set the trolley poles back a few feet. The hole for the new pole had been dug, and the pole, a great, heavy affair of steel, lay on the ground ready to be installed. In other days it would have taken a whole gang of men with pike poles and ropes and a derrick to put the thing in place. But, on this occasion, while the gang looked on–and drew no pay for looking–a long-nosed machine on a truck pushed its way up to the pole, swung the thing into the air, lodged it into the hole and straightened it up to true. One man operated the machine, another operated the truck, a third saw that the pole was straight up and down. The machine did the work, the men pulled levers, and the unemployed looked on.

A little later another machine appeared on the job–a cement mixer on a truck. Inside a tank were cement and water and a navvy jack, and great steel arms moved round and round, stirring up the mess.

When all was ready, the truck backed up to the pole, a chute was adjusted, a trap was opened and the liquid concrete, with a little help from a couple of shovels, flowed down into the hole and filled it up. A couple of men on the truck and a couple of men below–five minutes' work and it was all over. In other days the same number of men with barrows and shovels would have been at the job for an hour or two. We are living in a mechanical age, in which the machine does the work and men work the machine; and at times it appears as though the machine is taking the bread out of the men's mouths. It seemed so on Cambie Street yesterday, as the machines handled the pole and the unemployed stood by. But that was by no means the whole story. What made it necessary to plant a new pole? The traffic on Cambie Street. And this traffic is made up of motor cars–machines. And what is the function of the pole? To hold up a trolley wire for the operation of the streetcar–a machine. Had we been back in the times, a couple of generations ago–before the motor car or the streetcar–the pole, if erected, would have been erected by hand labour and the cement would have been mixed by hand and shovelled into the hole. No doubt, more men would have been employed. But there wouldn't have been any pole, because there would have been no need for it. So there wouldn't have been any unemployment at all in connection with it. Whatever employment there was in connection with the Cambie Street pole was the indirect result of a machine-created demand.

Machines are accused of destroying employment. No doubt they do. But they make more than they destroy. Like the Mississippi or the Peace or any other river with banks easily worn away, machinery is continually pulling down and building up. It destroys to create, and it creates only to destroy again. Those who benefit by the creation are happy for the time, but it is small satisfaction to those whose employment is destroyed to know that employment for someone else is being built up somewhere else.

## ✢ MACHINES AND MEN ✢

We are told that during the period from 1899 to 1919 the wages of workers increased 11 per cent, but in the ten years from 1919 to 1929 they increased 53 per cent. In 1918 it took one man all day to make 40 electric light bulbs, but the very next year a machine came along that turned out 73,000 bulbs in twenty-four hours. Each of these machines threw 992 men out of work. In boot and shoe manufacture, 100 machines take the place of 25,000 men. In the manufacture of razor blades, one man now turns out 32,000 blades in the same time that it took in 1913 to manufacture 500 blades. In automobile factories the same thing is in evidence. In one case 200 men are turning out between 7,000 and 9,000 frames a day. President [William] Green of the American Federation of Labor says that the trouble is that that country needs 6,000,000 new jobs. During the last ten years the increase in population has brought over 5,500,000 more persons who want jobs, while the jobs in manufacturing plants have decreased by 585,000.

## ✦ ENFORCED IDLENESS ✦

This is what impressed me most in my talk with the men in the jungle. The demoralizing effect of forced idleness, nothing to do, and all day and night to do it in. The daily talk with the low-down characters and the awful helplessness of their position made them feel: "What is the use of trying to find work; better to stay right here in the dump." And so in a land which needs the work of strong men, they are forced, by circumstances over which they have no control, to deteriorate into idleness. The softening process sets in, their physical, moral, and social fibre decays.

## ✦ SINS OF THE HOBO ✦

Sin is a theological term and literally means "missing the mark." This can be well applied to the homeless man, because of all classes of men, he has most certainly in more ways than one "missed the mark."

Sin may be classed under different headings. There are sins of the mind, dispositions of the heart, and sins of the flesh. If I read my New Testament aright, I find that Jesus condemned strongly the sins of hypocrisy, selfishness, covetousness and lying. On the other hand, while never condoning, He always spoke with a kinder tone in his voice when dealing with the sins of the flesh, as the example of the Woman of Samaria, Mary of Magdalene, and others. The sins of the hobo belong to the latter class.

## ✦ THE HOBO AND ALCOHOL ✦

After I had given an address one night in one of our churches in which I had pointed out the condition of these men, a lady called me the next day and, in a spirit of great indignation, declared that these men wasted their substance in riotous living and that was the reason why they were so hard up. She quoted for example one of our leading statesmen, a very wealthy man, who said: "In all his life he had never touched alcohol." "Now," she said, "see how rich he is."

It made my blood boil that anyone could be so ignorant and blind as to make such a statement. We must acknowledge there is a certain element of truth in the charge, but during the present emergency these men made very little money, either in the bush, the mine, or the harvest field, to spend in riotous living.

I always think of the experience of the Prophet Ezekiel when writing about the life of the exiled people in Babylon. He was a wise man, and in order to interpret the feelings of all the exiles properly he went down and lived among them and said: "I sat where they sat."

Can you imagine the feelings of these homeless men when they have a few dollars to spend? For months they may have been working in a construction camp, or in a mine, miles from civilization. The Church has shown little interest in them apart from the fact that some church members may have invested their money in the project on which they are working, and they are looking for their dividends in return. The human element does not appeal to the average investor even among some of the church members. It is none of their business, and in that way they salve their consciences and thank God they are not as other men.

The Shantyman's Mission may have an itinerant colporteur calling once a month, holding a service in the bunkhouse, taking a collection and then passing on.

The Frontier College may have a student working during the day and helping the men, and in his spare hours teaching them English and other elementary subjects.

There is a hungering in their hearts for fellowship, and out in the bush, down in the mine, below decks in a scorching stokehold, or out in the fields, they are counting the days when they will be able to make town and have a real good time, blowing their money and then, after a rest, back to the camp again to make more money and do the same again.

Now let us look at the situation. When the hobo comes to town, organized religion means little or nothing to him, but the saloon keeper, the prostitute, and the gambling den, they are all set to rob him of his hard-earned money. Because he hears no other invitation he follows their leadership and lets go. We blame the hobo, but put yourself in his place and what would you do? If you have done nothing to help him fight his battle, make life a little more pleasant by showing a friendly hand, you have no right to throw stones at him when he follows the wrong course.

He will drink while his money lasts and, like the Prodigal, will have no lack of friends. Then when his money is gone the saloon-keeper or the beer parlour proprietor and all the others get rid of him quick. He will endeavour to prolong the debauch by begging from his associates, then, when he has exhausted his efforts, he returns to work, a sadder, but unfortunately, not a wiser man.

One of the most dangerous drinking habits of the hobo is that of drinking canned heat. It is cheap, easy of access, gives a real kick and makes a good finish when it kills them off. They will smuggle it into lodging houses, rip the sheets and pillow cases and squeeze the alcohol out of the wax and drink it. The latest I have heard of is that some of them spread it on bread and eat it like a sandwich. It makes them blind, it makes them mad, and finally they take the count.

A man has gone very low down when he turns to canned heat to satisfy that awful craving for liquor, and he becomes what the hoboes term "a rummy stiff."

Yet it is scientifically true that the hobo who comes in for an occasional spree once or twice a year is less an alcoholic than the moderate drinker who has his tote of liquor every day. Out in the woods, where the perspiration flows freely, he cleans his body of the vile poisons and regains his balance again. Not so with the moderate drinker. He keeps on till his liver is as hard as nails, and then something happens and he is given a nice funeral, and a preacher is called in to speak nice words that don't mean a thing.

We must not blame the hobo when we remember the moments of utter loneliness that fill his heart, but rather let us lay the blame at the door of an indifferent, self-centred society that refuses to deal with this problem, or at the door of the organized church that has allowed, by its moral and spiritual laziness, the liquor interests to fasten their fangs on the body politic, or at the door of the politicians, who have been and are still, on their own confession, fattening themselves on the brewer's "Pap" and making themselves the ready tools of the liquor interests.

Hoboes, like all others who fall into the habits of intemperance, are the victims of a social order which, by its selfishness, refuses to deal with the traffic by the only known remedy, prohibition of the manufacture, sales and exportation of the cursed stuff.

## ✳ THE HOBO AND GAMBLING ✳

The old desire to get something for nothing makes a tremendous appeal to the homeless man, as it does to other individuals in society. The reckless, free, roving type of life encourages this habit. If he has no one to direct his leisure hours in the camp, he is bound to fall a victim to one evil habit or another. The flare of the white lights in the city, the pool room, with their back parlours, the numerous devices and traps set for these unfortunate men, make a tremendous appeal to him, and he readily falls a victim. It is tragic to listen to many of these men as they recite the story of their experiences. With some, experience is the only school by which they will learn.

## ⁓ THE SLANG OF THE HOBO ⁓

In the course of time, there has grown up an extensive vocabulary of very expressive terms used by these Knights of the Rods, thus forming a language all their own, just as the gypsies of Europe and America have a dialect peculiar to themselves. In order to express their feelings on all manner of subjects and situations, the hoboes have coined these phrases. They have been passed on from one jungle to another, and now are recognized as part of their daily slang. We have already described the difference between the hobo, the tramp and the bum; the bum loafs and sits, the tramp loafs and walks, but the hobo moves, works, and is clean.

*Bo* is short for hobo. I read recently where an endeavour was made to trace the origin of the word to the American Civil War. When soldiers walking through the country were asked where they were going, they would reply, "Homeward bound." This became abbreviated to hobo.

The *boomer* is a man who has a trade but cannot stay long in one place and so keeps moving about. This type of worker has played an important part in the development of Canada. This man has the skill but lacks the stick-to-it-iveness, and so, with a streak of wanderlust in his blood, he prefers to keep moving from job to job.

*Shorty* is the fellow who stands over six feet, and because of his size he is generally addressed by his fellow hoboes as Shorty. If a hobo blows into the jungle with red hair, he is called *Ginger*, and answers to that name as his mother would call him George. If any fellow lets it be known that his name is Miller, they forget that name and call him *Dusty*.

A *moocher* is a man who begs from people in the street. The *dummy* is one who has studied the art of playing dumb. The *blinker* is a man who stands and begs because he is blind, but not so blind as to know when a phoney coin is being given to him. *Canned heat artists* or *white-lined stiffs* are the names given to the fellows who drink the deadly wood alcohol. The *flopper* is the man you see on the edge of the curb, selling some kind of wares, or just begging.

A *flop* is a bed, and with the added adjective *lousy* is one of the strongest terms in the language of the hobo. The hobo, because he is clean, detests vermin, while the bum always feels at home with a few fleas on his shirt to keep him busy and remind him that he is not all bum. *Peg* is the name applied to the fellow who has lost a foot. *Stick* is the name given to the man who has lost a leg; and so on the list goes in a most interesting and striking manner. Every day some new term is being coined, while the old ones are being forgotten.

The hobo is an expert at the coming of new and expressive swear words, and when angered he can make the air so blue with the language that even the Devil himself would blush to hear. It would not be wise to repeat them in a story such as this, but it arouses a very interesting question. What is a swear word? And by what law of association do we measure them? There are words that reveal the vulgar and coarse mind and nature. Again there are words that reveal the perverted nature, having reference to obscene ideas in the mind of man. They come from a polluted nature and, let me remark here, they are not confined to the hobo, but reveal the diseased minds which are also to be found in the ranks of the intelligentsia.

There are other words that rise to the lips in moments of stress and anger. You will hear them used in the most select society because when the heart is evil, and the mind polluted, dress and environment are only secondary things.

The hobo expresses himself in a very frank and candid manner. The name of God and the name of Jesus are often on his lips, and are used without any thought of their higher spiritual relationship. Just a word with no suggestion or thought of reverence on the part of the user.

The hobo is no worse than some so-called respectable people who take the name of God in vain and yet make a profession of religion. Both need to be told that it is a sin to take the name of God in vain. You can imagine better than I would dare to describe what obscene thoughts and expressions would come from a group of men living as these homeless men are compelled to do, away from all the finer contacts of life, with all restraints and inhibitions broken down. Let us not condemn them unless we know all the experiences through which they may have passed.

The sin of profanity, the sin of vulgarity, and the sins of the flesh are all expressed in the vocabulary of the hobo, but let him who is without sin cast the first stone.

## ✥ THE SEX LIFE OF THE HOBO ✥

Being human, there are moments in his life when the hobo hungers and craves for the fellowship and intimate association of a good woman.

We must remember that most of these men had a home and a mother. They oftentimes think but rarely speak unless asked a question about them. We noticed that while we were serving the meals at the church, the men appreciated the kindly services of the women of the church.

More than once I have heard the women say: "That boy just makes me think of my own." And I have not the slightest doubt that the hobo often said he was reminded of his own mother by contact with a Christian woman.

Every city has its special attraction for these men, when they come to town after being away for months at a time from the contact of any women. You can well imagine the fight he has against temptation. In the army and navy, certain regulated areas are set apart for soldiers and sailors, and a certain amount of protection provided by medical inspection, which is more of a sham than a reality.

The hobo takes his chance, and while the money lasts and he has a good suit, he can pick and choose the young and more attractive women who ply their evil trade; but when he is penniless, and ragged, he associates with the lowest of the low. Soon or late the homeless man finds himself the victim of a loathsome venereal disease. At first he fails to recognize how serious it is. He listens to the advice of some old reprobate and soon finds himself in a terrible plight. The door of the social clinic is rarely darkened by the homeless man. When the disease is in an active state he becomes a menace to all with whom he associates. He may go into a camp and before his condition is discovered, a number of other men, through drinking utensils, towels, etc., may be seriously affected.

There is another real problem in the life of the homeless man or in a group of men who assemble together. By experience he has learned the dangers of infection from the common prostitute, and so the practice of homosexuality has come into vogue. This situation presents a real menace for the unwary youth who, in the spirit of adventure, boards a freight train to see the country. He is immediately spotted by one of these old hardened rascals, who will worm himself into the good graces of the boy and keep him for his own unlawful use, and he will be ready to fight for the ownership of the unfortunate youth.

We had a case of this nature in our work. A young lad who had been coming to our church, had taken sick and was not able to come for his daily rations of food. We investigated and found the lad was being held in fear and bondage in the cabin of one of these depraved men. The case was reported and the police took action and set him free. They have a special name for this type of man; he is called a *wolf.*

What would you expect from the life of these homeless men than a perverted sex nature. They are far removed from the influence of pure and true womanhood except as they meet them in a mission or welfare work. The jokes, stories, and conversation, the class of literature he may read, all tend to feed the lower passions of their nature and fill the imagination with thoughts that breed an immoral life.

Can we condemn him as we sing our hymns, read our Bibles, say our prayers, and have our association with the fine noble Christian women we have as mothers, sisters and sweethearts? When we judge these men on the question of their sexual life, let us remember the background of their existence and the unnatural life which, by the laws of choice and necessity, they are compelled to live.

## ⚜ THE RELIGION OF THE HOBO ⚜

It may surprise you to know that, from personal experience, I have found a considerable number of these men have had a religious background. Sometimes it was an early contact with Sunday school or church membership. Again it was the remembrance of the religion of a good mother that impressed them most.

There are few churches engaged directly in the work among homeless men. This important task is unfortunately left to missions of a very mixed and oftentimes questionable nature.

Their theology and their understanding of the problem, as well as their methods, are sometimes very wide of the mark. In every city you will find at least one centre where work of this nature is carried on during the winter months.

The religion of the hobo is very simple and very direct. He has his own thoughts about God and man, and salvation and Heaven. In the midst of his loneliness, he has his times of serious and earnest heart searching, and many a prayer crudely formed rises from the lips of these homeless men like the sob of a wounded heart, when they realize that every man's hand is against them, and in the words of the Psalmist, "No man careth for my soul."

There is a turning point in the life of these homeless men when they will either maintain their self-respect, or they will follow the course of least resistance and go down. What a difference it would make to a man, if at that moment in his life he could come in contact with a real friend who would stand by him and steady him in the crisis.

It is the absolute sense of hopelessness that fills the hearts of these homeless men in times like these that drives them to the depths of despair.

How real are the words of the Master when He reminds us that He came to seek and save that which was lost. There is a unique opportunity for the church to have some real constructive programme on behalf of these men. In every city you will find a number of downtown churches. They have been left as the tide mark of business and industry has moved inward and the people have gradually moved outward to the suburban areas.

Many of these churches have been sold for large sums of money and the unearned increment has gone to build "elaborated quarries," as John McNeill, the famous Scottish evangelist, called them, in the beautiful suburban areas.

Surely it should be apparent now that if cathedrals and costly churches could have saved the world, then Europe would have been Christian long ago. God is not interested in the externals of religion, but He is still vitally interested in men and women.

Too many of our modern churches have seized the opportunity to get something for nothing. They have gambled in real estate, moved into a new locality, built beautiful churches, called a safe preacher and then invited God to come and worship with them on condition that He would not interfere with their way of running religion. In the meantime, factories, warehouses, picture shows or beer saloons have taken the place of the church in these downtown areas. The United Church of Canada has seen a vision and the great opportunity and responsibility of holding these strategic centres for the Kingdom of God, believing that it is a real home mission work. They have through the Home Mission department put into every centre across the Dominion of Canada the best possible equipment, the best possible leadership, thus strengthening the forces of righteousness to meet and fight the forces of evil, and to reclaim broken humanity and restore it at the Cross of God in the name of Jesus of Nazareth.

### Souls for Doughnuts: The Tramp's Confession

We huddled in the mission,
Fer it was cold outside,
And listened to the preacher
Tell of the Crucified.

Without a sleety drizzle
Cut deep each ragged form,
An' so we stood the talkin'
Fer shelter from the storm.

They sang of Gods and Angels,
An' Heaven's eternal joy,
An' things I stopped believin'
When I was still a boy.

They spoke of good an' evil,
An' offered savin' grace,
An' some showed love for mankind
A shinin' in their face.

An' some their graft was workin,'
The same as me and you;

But some was urgin' on us
What they believed was true.

We sang an' dozed an' listened,
But only feared, us men,
The time when, service over,
We'd have to mooch again.

An' walk the icy pavements,
An' breast the snowstorm gray,
Till the saloons was opened,
An' there was hints of day.

So, when they called out, "Sinners,
Won't you come?" I came–
But in my face was pallor,
An' in my heart was shame–
An' so fergive me, Jesus,
Fer mockin' of Thy Name.

Fer I was cole an' hungry;
They gave me food and bed
After I kneeled there with them,
An' many prayers was said,

An' so fergive me, Jesus,
I didn't mean no harm–
Fer outside it was zero,
An' inside it was warm.

Yes, I was cold an' hungry,
An' oh, Thou Crucified,
Thou Friend of all the Lowly,
Fergive the lie I lied.

From The Hobo by Prof. Nels Anderson.

The Gospel ought to be free in every sense of the word. Nothing of any real religious value can come from the practice of holding men for three hours in a service on condition that if they sat through the service they would receive doughnuts and coffee. You can well imagine a group of men on a cold winter night, seeking the warmth of the Mission room sleeping and dozing, while the preacher gets excited about hell-fire and brimstone, the only effect of which is to create a mental picture and make the men feel a little warmer. Then at the close to call out for those who will stand up for Jesus to come forward. Many of the men are forced into hypocrisy because of these tactics, and some of them are converted at every meeting they attend. Such methods as these cause a man to lose his self-respect and to be insincere. My policy would be to give the man his meal first and his medicine after.

True religion can be put into the service which will be appreciated by these men without holding the fear of hell-fire and brimstone over their heads when many of them have had enough of hell in their life to last them for a long time to come.

I always remember Gypsy Smith telling of an enthusiastic worker in one of the rest camps during the war. The men had just come down from the lines and they were cold, wet and hungry. The young enthusiast shouted out, "Just a minute boys, we will thank Jesus for this." A voice called back, "Never mind, boys, put Jesus in the coffee."

It is true these men need religion, but not so much a religion of hell-fire as some think they do. They will take a lot from a man if they know he is sincere and can make good. The story is told of John Wesley who was on one occasion invited to preach before a company of the peers of the realm in England. He chose for his text "O generation of vipers who hath warned you to flee from the wrath to come?"

At the close, one of them took John Wesley severely to task

for having dared to preach such a sermon on such a text to such a distinguished gathering. "You should have preached that sermon in Newgate Jail." "No, my lord," came the response. "If I had been in Newgate Jail, I would have preached on the text, 'Behold the Lamb of God hath taken away the sins of the world.'"

These men appreciate a downright sincere, earnest Gospel message and many of them have found Jesus and experienced the power of a new life, and have made good. One of our young students found himself confronted with a real problem in one of the camps in British Columbia. He wanted to hold a service in the bunkhouse and he was told it would be all right if he would preach a sermon from the text that would be written on the wall next Sunday. The student arrived and the men swarmed into the bunkhouse, and one fellow got up and wrote on the wall these words: "To hell with the church." A loud laugh greeted this announcement, and all eyes were fixed on the student. For a moment he halted. Then, as if by inspiration, he wrote these words: "The gates of hell shall not prevail against it." He won out and the men appreciated his services every time he came to camp.

A simple direct message, the old familiar hymns, an earnest prayer will break down the strongest resistance of the hardest hobo, and be more effective than all the logic and argument of the most eloquent preacher and all the hell-fire and brimstone of the fanatic.

These old words are still true:

Down in the human heart, crushed by the tempter,
Feelings lie buried that grace can restore;
Touched by a loving hand, wakened by kindness,
Chords that were broken, will vibrate once more.

"Do you think religion does these men any good?" I am asked. "Of course I do," I reply. "'The Son of Man came not to be ministered unto, but to minister and to give his life a ransom for

59

many,' and 'The Son of Man came to seek and to save that which was lost.'"

These men, our unfortunate brothers, are lost to those who love them, to society, to themselves, and to God, in their present condition. I believe that Jesus can help them and that He is interested in them and that His power alone can keep them.

Therefore as a minister, I must try to help them in every way possible to get a hold on life and from experience in dealing with men, I know that the Gospel of the Grace of God, revealed through the life of Jesus, is able to save to the uttermost.

## ✢ KAGAWA VISITS THE JUNGLE ✢

When Dr. Toyohiko Kagawa, of Japan, visited the city of Vancouver in August of last year he called to see me to discuss our work in First United Church and to learn something about the slum conditions in the city of Vancouver.

The name of Kagawa is a name respected among Christians and non-Christians of every land. He is a man who believes that the Gospel of Jesus is a social Gospel. The work among the outcast classes of Japan, the sacrifices he has made on their behalf, are a challenge to our Christian faith. Kagawa said: "I believe in the Gospel of social righteousness. The power of love alone can bring economic, social, political, and religious emancipation."

During the course of our conversation, I suggested he would come with me down to the jungles. He readily responded. When we reached the jungles, we moved about, speaking to the different groups. Kagawa sat down in one of those rude shelters beside a fellow-countryman of my own, a Scotsman, and talked to him about his life and experiences. I only wish I had had a camera in my hand at that time. The words of the Prophet Ezekiel flashed to my mind: "I sat where they sat." Here was a man, this noble Christian gentleman who has given his life and his means in the interest of the poor and underprivileged in his own native country of Japan, and who has lived and worked amid the slums, accustomed to scenes of degradation, dirt and disease, but a man with a burning passion in his soul to help his fellows. He said to me: "We have the same conditions in Japan, but I am working hard to clean them out, so that we will have no jungles in Japan." The men appreciated what he had to say to them, especially when I told them who he was and what he was trying to do, and that he was a friend of humanity.

### ❖ HOW THE HOBO TRAVELS ❖

When you go to the booking agent at the railway station and pay your money, he gives you a ticket in exchange. It may be a piece of cardboard or a yard of perforated paper which is your passport until you reach your destination. The hobo dispenses with all such preliminaries. A ticket office is unnecessary to him, and he makes his plans without even consulting a timetable. When he decides on a destination, which he may never reach, but that does not worry him, he finds out what he can, not from the official agent, but from the latest arrival in the jungle over that route.

He learns what the prospects are for work, how the chances are for getting by for food on the Stem, where the jungles are located; he will find out how the *bulls* (policemen) are acting along the line, the number who are making the grade, and all the other necessary information which will assist him in reaching the place where he fancies he would like to be. If you asked him just why he wanted to get to Montreal or Vancouver, he would only give you a flimsy excuse. The fact would be that the spirit of wanderlust is moving in his blood, and he feels he must go. He travels light unless he is a *bundle-* or *blanket stiff,* and rolling all his possessions together, he starts for the open road. Should he want to get there in a hurry he dispenses with all these extras, puts his razor and strop in his pocket, a box of matches, and some tobacco if he is lucky enough to have any, and he hits the trail.

With a wistful look at the campfire, a side glance at the ramshackle which has been his home for a week or more, and a word to his vagabond companions, who may be too busy, intent on doing nothing in particular to take any notice of him, he slides out into the night.

He wanders down to the railway yards, keeping his eye open for the policemen, as he does not desire any free lodging at the expense of the government.

When he arrives at the railway yards, he does not enquire which train is pulling out. There are other figures stealing along the side of the tracks evidently bent on the same purpose as himself. No word is spoken. Long experience has taught the hobo that it is better to keep his mouth shut until the train is moving, and then there is lots of time to find out who's who in Hobo Land.

The men disappear into the dark shadows along the track. The searchlight of the switching engine as it rounds the corner reveals a dozen or more men who run like hunted animals to escape the light. At last the long heavy freight, eastbound or westbound, begins to move slowly out of the yards. Immediately out of all the dark recesses the men rush forward and climb onto the rods.

Those who are experts get on first; the *greenhorns* and *lame birds* hesitate and are helped by their companions. The train is gaining speed every minute and usually there are a few that are left; the old men, the cripples, and those who, at the last moment, changed their minds. The 10:10, which leaves Vancouver for the East every night, carries a goodly number of uninvited guests of the CPR.

The following story gives you a very vivid impression of the experiences of one of these men who, for the first time, rides the rods. He called at our office and I had a conversation with him, and the impressions he has set forth I am passing on to you. It was published in the Vancouver *Daily Province.*

## ⚘ JOURNAL OF AN AMATEUR BOXCAR TOURIST ⚘

Ten o'clock one evening saw me in the yards of the CNR at Edmonton, waiting for the westbound freight.

I had never before ridden a freight, nor travelled without money; I had not the haziest idea of what to do. I lurked in the shadows, feeling like a criminal hoping to escape notice. I heard the monotonous beat of an engine steaming up somewhere.

A number of men materialized out of the darkness and approached the line of empty boxcars. Three of them came up to me and in low tones asked when the train left. "Any time now," I replied. "She's due out at 10:30."

"We got in this morning from Montreal," volunteered one. "Things are tough there, a sight worse than here. There's hundreds riding into Winnipeg every day. They jungle up right by the tracks, and the railroad police don't interfere with them. But the town's hostile, all the same—pinch you on the streets for vag even if you ain't doing nothing. Everybody's broke, and you can't get a bite to eat without money. There's a bunch of men there waiting for trouble to start, and, believe me, if anything started there that town would sure hum. Provincials couldn't handle it—it'd be a militia job."

"Provincials!" sneered the other. "They're scared stiff half the time. They do their best to let on they're King Tut, but they don't know which way to jump. They can't run us out of the jungles, there'd be a riot if they did. Sometimes they pinch a few 'boes, just to show they ain't scared, but it don't go. We ride the trains as if we owned 'em, and the train crews don't bother. There's too many men on the road now for police control. There's thousands in Montreal; Toronto's full of 'em; there's an awful big bunch going through Winnipeg day and night, and Vancouver's just a blamed summer resort for all the hoboes in Canada."

A diminutive youth, with a pack nearly as big as himself, glanced around apprehensively.

"There's a bull over there," indicating where a lantern swung through the gloom. ·

"Sure," scoffed the first speaker, a raw-boned, red-bearded man of middle age. "He's looking for hobes, but he's careful to look in all the wrong places and keep out of dark corners. The other night they pinched eight. There was a hundred and fifty on the train, and the bulls nabbed eight and beat it to the jailhouse before they got cleaned up on."

He spat into the darkness contemptuously.

The locomotive by the roundhouse hooted twice and began to draw abreast. I went over to the track, wondering whether I should jump clean on or blunder clumsily; a fleeting vision of steel rails and rumbling wheels rose before me. The next moment I had jumped and was mounting the stepladder to the roof of a boxcar. I made my way along the boxcars to the tender, which offered shelter from the wind.

At least 20 hoboes were seated on the roofs of the first few cars and two or three were already on the tender. As I felt my way uncertainly from boxcar to tender, one of them rose and assisted me to clamber on.

"Where you heading for, young feller?" "Kamloops," I replied. "What time do we make Edson?" "'Bout 4 o'clock in the morning; gonna be a cold run. There aren't any empty boxcars on. There's never any empties on this line, but coming from Vancouver there's plenty on the seaboard freight."

We were soon clear of the light of town. The train roared through the darkness. The cold began to penetrate. Cinders, like hail, finding their way down my neck, added considerably to my discomfort.

Two hours must have passed thus when we halted. I heard the tanks filling with water. Before I could rise to my feet an overflow had soaked my legs.

I knew it would take some time before I should be dry. I no longer felt so sure of finding work; I realized I had only 40 cents in my pocket and not much food in my pack. I dreamed of a warm bed and clean sheets. Damp cinders crunched as I moved. What on earth had sent me off on this mad venture? I was a fool; I wished there were no such thing as freight trains, and half resolved to go back to Edmonton next morning. At last, weariness triumphed over cold and wet; I fell asleep.

I awoke at Edson, stiff with cold. I descended from the tender and dropped to the ground heavily. It was necessary to circle the railway yards and wait an hour or more for the train to leave.

Numbers of other drifters were around me, grimy, unshaven; ordinary workmen out of a job. A few bore the stamp of the waster. One meets on the road many of these, and pathetic indeed is their lot, meriting pity rather than blame. Worthless, drifting vagabonds, dirty and dishonest, they never know the joy of home nor the respect of their fellow-men. They drift with the current, hither and thither; they know nothing of the pleasure of a task fulfilled. The sun rose, driving out the damp chill. As we lay sunning ourselves a short stocky fellow approached and hailed us cheerfully. He carried a blackened lard pail full of steaming tea. Squatting on the ground, he chatted between sips. He started over to where a long line of hoboes were straggling off the jungles.

"This country," he said, "has gone on the bum right. When I was in Montreal last Monday, there were suits for sale at $2.50; Russian stuff. It's Russia that's put the rest of the world on the blink."

The man next to me grunted. "Yes, and if Russia goes on with her Five-Year Plan, she's going to stagnate Canada. Russia's dumping her stuff at less than a Chinaman's price. We can't hope to compete, even in our own markets, and she'll go on dumping till Canada is flat. That's what Russia's aiming at—to bust the rest of the world. These countries are importing cheap Russian goods, and then their own people get thrown out of work and gotta be kept. Lookit Britain; we lost our trade there. Russian grain and furs and lumber have put Canadian produce out of the field. Canada's poor and Britain can't sell us her manufactures. And where the heck is Britain? Over two million out of work and on the dole. 'Tain't doing nobody no good."

The tea drinker took up the chorus: "Lookit me," he requested proudly, "lookit me. I ain't looking for work. 'Cos why? 'Cos there ain't none. They've abolished work. There's three classes of people getting by doing nothing today. There's your politician, who's all hot air and nothing else. There's your poor guy in the klink—three squares a day and a flop and no work. Then there's your tramp, maybe three squares a day and maybe a flop, and surely no work."

"Yeah, maybe," growled one. "But more often you pull your belt in three times a day and whistle a tune for luck."

"Not if you're a good tramp; not if you're a good tramp," replied Shorty quickly.

"You can't work; you gotta be a tramp. They've abolished work. I ain't worked for nearly a year. Sure, we all want work and wages, but nobody will employ us. So we gotta be tramps. You can eat good if you know how. If you're going to be a tramp, be a good tramp."

With this he finished his tea, smacked his lips appreciatively and hung the blackened lard pail on his pack. "Well, so long, buddies. See you all in Vancouver next fall."

At six o'clock the train departed, bearing a heavy cargo of men in addition to its legitimate freight. At Jasper we walked through the town to miss the yards. Soot and cinders had made me filthy; my eyes were sore and bloodshot. Young men, neat and lean, passed me with a disgusted casual glance. My humiliation was far less to be endured than any of the hardships of the road.

Leaving Jasper, I rode on the roof of a boxcar the whole day to Blue River, stretched out at full length with my blankets beneath my head, enjoying the hot sun and the ever-changing beauty of the country. A supply of tobacco encouraged the genial mood. If one could but live on scenery, that valley would be the end of all troubles. The hoboes sat in little groups, chatting and smoking, or lay at full length drowsing. Many bore the marks of privation and suffering. Gaunt, emaciated, bleary-eyed, sunk in the depths of oblivion, they twitched and grunted uneasily, or stared with hopeless eyes into the distance. I offered one a cigarette, and he clawed at it wolfishly, with hooked lean fingers like the talons of a hawk. A look of gratitude lightened his features, and soon the man was puffing contentedly. Wherever these men collect, the question foremost in their minds is "How long is it going to last?"

Ever ready to discuss conditions, to regard the question from every angle, to consider the diverse opinions of their fellow wayfarer, for the most part they entertain far sounder views on the present crisis than any smug armchair theorist.

Freedom of speech is observed in these debates. One man has a view which he expresses, free from interruption. His opinion is then challenged or endorsed, as the case may be, by others present. They see before them the long black void of dreary months.

Sunset and Blue River. Missing two meals left me giddy, and the night's chill made me shudder. I slept that night on the floor of an empty boxcar. At Kamloops junction, just before dawn, I left the train and made camp by the North Thompson River. Here I tarried till the following afternoon, then set out for Kamloops to get the night freight to Kelowna. On the way I met a railway policeman, who enquired whither I was bound.

On hearing I was planning to take the Canadian National from Kamloops to Kelowna, he said: "You won't get there by Canadian National. The CNR doesn't go till Friday. (It was now Monday.) You had better take the Canadian Pacific Railway and go by way of Sicamous."

I thanked him. I passed a few hoboes, some of whom were bound for Vancouver. "Why Vancouver?" I queried of one pair.

"It's as good a place as any. This is our sixth trip between Montreal and Vancouver now. We can't stay in one place; the bulls send us out of town. We gotta keep goin'." Despite the disguising grin and the hard lines about his mouth, the face and voice of the speaker suggested extreme youth.

"How old are you, youngster?" I asked.

"Fifteen, and this here's my kid brother. We're travellin' together."

"Where are you goin'?" I questioned.

"Oh, jus' travellin'," he replied, hopelessly.

It is an interesting spectacle to watch a freight leave any of the main line divisional points. As the engine *highballs* and draws out of the yards, one may see fifty men or more leave their various cubbyholes on either side of the line and climb the train, swarming over its entire length, seeking the best places in which to settle for the journey. The train crews are of the opinion that if they attempted to eject the hoboes they would be mobbed. The average hobo is inoffensive and law-abiding, but, urged by hunger, he may pilfer gardens and orchards for food.

Generally, he deplores the cases of house-breaking and shoplifting of which one reads today. He deems it better to rob a bank than a small storekeeper.

Many hold biased opinions on politics. Socialism and capitalism, the very meaning of which words they fail to grasp. Some are frankly "Red." Usually the ne'er-do-wells hold the most radical ideas, but these form a small minority and receive but little attention.

The better-class man on the road, of whom there are thousands today, strongly resents any criticism of Canada. He is opposed to revolution. One large factor in the cause of dissatisfaction is the employment of foreigners in the face of the unemployment in this country. The common belief is that wherever it is possible those who are employing men hire foreigners rather than Canadians. I am not prepared to discuss this point, but after two weeks of travelling I have seen comparatively few foreigners on the freights. Nearly all are English-speaking people.

At the CNR depot an obliging *brakie* told me that a train left for Kelowna on the Canadian National that night before 11 p.m. I was accosted by a railway policeman. "Where are you going?" he barked. "Kelowna, CN, tonight's freight," I replied laconically. "Yes," that's right, Mac," said the policeman, with a change of tone. "Can't get there by CPR, you know. We don't go that way."

"I could take the CPR by way of Sicamous, couldn't I?"

"Sure. You could do that, but the train doesn't go till Friday. You better take the CN. It goes out tonight."

It was the same tune the CN policeman had given me. Somewhat puzzled, I wended my way to the CNR yards where, in an empty boxcar, I found shelter from the rain. Some other hoboes were already there. From them I sought explanations for the contradictions of the police.

"They're all like that," I was told. "The CN bulls tell you to go by CP and the CP bulls tell you to go by CN. Nobody wants us. Pretty soon they'll start a war to kill us all off. Jake with me. They didn't kill me in the last war. They're welcome to try again."

There seems to be a growing conviction that unless there is soon an improvement in conditions, a revolution will break out within the year. I doubt it. The Canadian is not a revolutionist.

There may be riots, perhaps serious ones, with the foreign population featuring largely in them, but the unemployed lack leadership, without which they can do little. Moreover, they do not incline towards violence and bloodshed. Being out of work does not transform them all from peaceful citizens to savages. Many are from the ranks of skilled craftsmen and others of similar standing. They are sufficiently well informed to realize that demonstrations and riots benefit them not at all. Of course, there are exceptions. There are also the dregs, who loaf around the cities like pariah dogs—a menace, but for their cowardice. They form but a small number.

These are my opinions, engendered during this rough journey which continued on through Kelowna, Penticton, Vernon and Ashcroft to Vancouver, with a little detour afoot along the Cariboo Trail. That and a night spent in the hills above Summerland were the only pleasant interludes along the way. I do not know what will happen next.

We have fixed up scores of men for the long journey across Canada. In the winter we provided them with warm clothing and food, and in the summer with a box of bread, cheese and hard-boiled eggs, to get them by until they can make their destination.

It has become one of the pastimes for the passengers on the TransCanada trains to count the hoboes on the freight cars. The largest number I have heard of was 252 on one train heading for the Coast.

Evidently the police have been given instructions to let them pass. The municipalities know that if they arrest these men and they are sent to jail, they would have to pay one dollar a head per day. The trainmen realize that this is a special emergency and until the Government announce a programme of works ready, they might as well let them come. It requires lots of nerve and stamina to stand the racket on a freight train, day and night, across Canada. Some of these men have no food when they start. They trust to luck and plan to live by begging at each divisional point on the way across. Those who are old hands and know the ropes get by, some of them in great style; but the other poor beggars have a rough time and often they are hungry.

There are many dangers to be faced, especially by those who want to make a fast trip; they climb up on the tenders of the passenger engine. About 12 or 13 men can lie there; they have to hold on like grim death, mile after mile. The old hands, as well as the greenhorns, must look out for the long tunnels. The smoke and gas overcome many of them. The plan is to soak their blanket or overcoat with water at the last divisional point and then when they reach the tunnel, they take the blanket and wrap it around their heads and keep it there until they can see light. Failure to do this may bring serious consequences on the individual through suffocation and danger of falling off.

There are no statistics available, but in the course of a year many of these men lose their lives and nothing much is heard of it. A large number of them are crippled, or *winged* as they call it, through having met with serious accidents, climbing on and jumping off moving trains. The hospital records in the cities and towns across Canada show a number of these homeless men who have met with serious accidents, which have cost them life and limb.

I remember one young lad, who fell between the tracks and had both legs cut off. Nobody knew about it and only by chance was he found a little later lying bleeding to death on the tracks. The only words he could utter in the hospital were, "My mother, my mother." He died a few days later, a fine wholesome looking boy. Friends got in touch with his mother in the Old Country, and the Sons of England took charge of the service and gave him a Christian burial, for which that mother will be forever grateful.

The body of Wilgot Lexen, cut in two, was found lying across the tracks of the Kettle Valley Railway in the tunnel half a mile west of Princeton. Lexen, who resided in the jungle west of the town, was unemployed for some time, but had just secured work with a pole gang. He was unmarried.

During the winter months, when some of them ride the rods, they suffer terribly through frozen feet and hands, and on more than one occasion they have been frozen to death. Others again have entered an open freight car which has been closed on them, and they have been unable to open it. After several days of terrible experiences they have been found half dead.

During the past year, when a vessel broke through the gates of one of the locks in one of the large canals, it was estimated that from one to 15 of these men were drowned, carried away by the rush of water that swamped them in their jungle. It is a hard way, and when men are young and vigorous, they can stand the racket; but soon they fall by the wayside and join the homeguard. Their travelling days are done and the last journey they make is the ride to the cemetery to be buried in a pauper's grave.

## ✢ THE HEALTH OF THE HOBO ✢

When you visit a jungle or meet these men on the street, at first glance they seem to be in good physical condition. The exposure to the weather has tanned their skins a deep brown. The human body has its limits of resistance and after years of abuse and neglect, many of them fall victims of diseases of different kinds. It is in the winter when they are forced by unemployment to live in these terrible jungles or in the lousy lodging houses where there is often no light or air in the winter months. The marvel to me is that they do not die off like flies.

TB takes the greatest toll of life. My heart goes out in sympathy for them when, in the bread line, I hear them coughing and coughing, many of them with little clothing on. We had instructions from the Health department to report any such cases and they usually took care of them. Rheumatism takes a very heavy

# JOBLESS DIE IN QUEBEC CRASH

## Deaths Estimated at From One to 18 in Disaster at Montreal

### CANAL GATE HIT

## Victims Swept to Doom as Steamer Collides With Lock Control

**Canadian Press Despatch**

MONTREAL, Aug. 2.—Loss of life for a number of unknown unemployed men, variously estimated at from one to 18, and a complete tie-up of the Lachine Canal on both sides resulted today when the river boat Rapids Prince crashed into the upper gate of Lock Two of the Canal.

The men, breakfasting and washing along the canal bank, were swept into the water. Many were rescued and immediately moved away. Police estimated 40 men were at the canal, of whom some 20 or more were saved. A sudden torrent of water, pouring through the broken gate, caused the fatalities.

All the canal department sheds and offices at the scene of the accident were carried away with the exception of two. Damage was roughly estimated at $300,000 and it was believed the canal would be tied up for two or three days or more.

toll of life among these men. Living in unhealthy surroundings, their feet soaking wet and their bodies drenched with rain, the disease lays hold on them and many of them suffer untold agony when they try to raise themselves from their beds. You do not have to ask them what is the matter, you can see it in their faces. It is evident there must be something wrong with a system in which we have manufactured so many shoes, so much clothing, grown so much wheat, caught so many fish, built so many houses, and yet human beings are in such dire need.

If foot and mouth disease breaks out in any section of the Dominion of Canada, the health authorities immediately take action to save the animals because they represent an investment of money, but when human beings are hungry and cold, sick and homeless, nobody cares except a comparatively few charitable institutions and individuals who have to urge the Government to do something on behalf of these unfortunate creatures. I am convinced it is time for a change in our social order.

## ⁕ INSANITY ⁕

This wandering, homeless life gets on the nerves of many of these men, especially if they have left a good home and they imagine they cannot go back. There is a deep sense of shame lingering in their hearts; some of them have prison records. In some cases the old home is gone, their parents are dead. Under disguise some of them have gone back to their old haunts and come away with that utter sense of loneliness in their hearts. There is nothing left in life, nobody cares; their hearts are hungering for friendship. Then something snaps. A man's chums find him chattering and laughing.

The police are called and they take him away. His travelling days are done. Behind the doors of the mental hospital he comes to the end of the long trail.

## *The Hobo's Last Lament*

Beside a Western water tank
One cold November day,
Inside an empty boxcar,
A dying hobo lay;
His old pal stood beside him,
With low and drooping head,
Listening to the last words,
As the dying hobo said:

"I am going to a better land,
Where everything is bright,
Where beef-stews grow on bushes,
And you sleep out every night,
And you do not have to work at all,
And never change your socks,
And streams of goodly whiskey
Come trickling down the rocks.

"Tell the bunch around the Market street,
That my face no more they'll view;
Tell them I've caught a fast freight,
And that I'm going straight on through.
Tell them not to weep for me,
No tears in their eyes must lurk;
For I'm going to a better land,
Where they hate the word called work.

"Hark! I hear her whistling,
I must catch her on the fly;
I would like one scoop of beer
Once more before I die."

The hobo stopped, his head fell back,
He'd sung his last refrain;
His old pal stole his coat and hat
And caught an eastbound train.

## ⚘ THE HOBO AND THE COMMUNIST ⚘

The hoboes, tramps and bums are the despair of the Communists. They do not know what to make of them. They will not respond to their passionate appeals. They just look and accept the inevitable, and so long as food and shelter are provided they are content. That, of course, is their loss.

I remember on one occasion, while visiting at a mental hospital, I saw a large number of the inmates all gathered together in the centre of the grounds. I asked the attendant what would happen if they made some plan of attack. He turned to me as he said: "There is no danger of that because they can never agree on anything. They are all individualists. Whatever action they might take would be the action of the individual and not the group." That same spirit prevails among the hoboes. They will talk about aims and objects and curse and damn the capitalist system, but when it comes to the actual working out of ideas, it is impossible to do anything with them. They have a feeling that every man's hand is against them. The boss, the Labour party, the Capitalist and the Communist are all trying to put something over on them, which they will not stand. To the hobo, all men are liars and he prefers to run his own show. He is a man without a job, a home, a cause or country.

He has no inclination to stay anywhere when the work is done. He fails to see that only by co-operative effort can he and his class clamber out of the bog of despair into which they have fallen. I have met the Communists in their operations among the men, in the church, in the jungle, and in the bread line.

One night we had a mass meeting of the men, when they asked me to address them. I made no bones about it, but informed them that, in my judgment, the solution of all our problems—social, economic and political—was to be found in the teachings of this old Book. I showed them that the Old Testament prophets, like Amos and Hosea, as well as the teachings of Jesus, stood for the very things they had in their platform, and that Jesus Himself was on the side of the outcast and the underprivileged members of society. They listened and never said a word. The Communists then wanted to talk, and I allowed them the floor. I have learned that it is a good safety valve, even in the church, to let them say their say. They sang "The Red Flag" and went quietly out of the church hall.

The Communists have come down to the jungles, men and women, and tried to stop us from feeding the men, but I have just kept on, said nothing, and fed the men. One day, they were distributing pamphlets down the bread line, containing some rebel stuff. I stood in full view of the long line of men. Putting one of the leaflets in my mouth, I said: "Look, fellows, you can't eat that," and then holding a loaf of bread in my hand, I said: "But you can eat this, and while the others are doing all the talking, I will do the feeding, and we will work together for a solution of our problems."

I would like to say this word, however: that I only wish the Christian Church could catch something of the spirit of missionary zeal that is burning so strong in the heart of the Communist. One day I was called upon to bury a young Ukrainian who had died. After I had pronounced the benediction, a young man named Mike jumped on top of the mound of earth and began to preach to his fellow countrymen with a zeal and enthusiasm I envied. They listened intently to what he had to say. When he had finished, I said: "Mike, what did you tell those people?" He said: "I told them that our young comrade was dead, but that we, the young workers of the world, must pledge our common loyalty and work for the revolution and the common cause of humanity." It is the old conflict between economic determinism and spiritual determinism. My own opinion is that there must be a *via media* between those two philosophies of life. That way has not yet been found, and so we have an over-emphasis on the one side or the other. There are those who declare that economic determinism determines everything. We have to recognize the fact that there is a great deal of truth in the statement. If you take sick, your economic standing will determine whether they put you in a private ward or in the basement of the hospital. It will determine whether you live in a beautifully appointed home, or try to bring up your family in a two-room tenement in the slums.

On the other hand, no matter how elaborate the home may be, or how great the salary, wages or income may be, if the moral and spiritual life of the individuals are not touched, they will, like the swine, "return to their wallowing in the mire, or, like the dog, to his vomit."

When the hobo stops his wandering and informs himself of these things, he will then be more receptive to new ideas. Meantime he is more interested in getting by at the job, along the stem, or in the jungles.

## ✦ THE NEXT STEP ✦

Church and state must face this problem of the homeless man with a new attitude and a strong determination to remedy the condition as far as possible. If this state of affairs is allowed to continue, and these thousands of homeless men drift to and fro across this Dominion of Canada, the future will bring a terrible harvest of wasted life. Passing resolutions at conferences, assemblies, and parliaments is not enough. There must be action on the part of the whole church and the municipal, provincial and federal authorities, because it is a national problem. It is not my purpose to lay down specific rules, theories and regulations, but rather to create a new attitude towards this problem.

As never before the attention of the world is being focused on the problem of unemployment, whether it affects the life of the family or the individual. I, for one, refuse to believe that with all our potential knowledge, skill and wisdom, this problem cannot be solved in this great Canada of ours.

The Church of Jesus Christ must put a new emphasis on the sacredness of personality, and any form of social legislation that prevents the full realization of that personality must be opposed. Selfishness and indifference on the part of the Christian Church are largely to blame for the present condition. We must learn to take Jesus seriously and apply the teachings of His Gospel to every phase of life.

In conclusion, I would quote part of a personal letter that I received from the Right Honourable Ramsay MacDonald. He says: "My message is that righteousness alone, in all its manifold expressions and applications exhalteth a nation, and that great wealth and material prosperity become burdens unless controlled by spiritual power. What the world needs today is the direction of that moral and spiritual power for the creation of a new Christian world order."

### ✢ THE JUNGLES IN DON VALLEY ✢
Here is a picture of one of the jungles in Toronto.
By Rev. Peter Bryce, D.D.

George Williams, Ray McCleary and Peter Bryce paid a neighbourly visit last night to our fellow-citizens in the Don Valley. We called first upon a group of twenty men in what appeared to me an empty brick kiln. There were that number of beds, made by the grouping of bricks, upon which were laid boards. Near each bed could be seen the occupant's clothing, severely limited, and his stock of groceries, also of Spartan proportions. A "homey" feeling was apparent. Two groups were having a cup of tea together. We received a kindly welcome and chatted together for a while. The uppermost question was about the camps. When are they going to open up? Men from Scotland, Ireland, England, and from various parts of Canada, were in this group.

We wandered outside, and found reclining against the kilns many men, all trying to make themselves comfortable for the night. By an open brazier with a bright light sat two men, one Irish, the other from Greece. The Greek was a friendly chap, eager to talk.

"This is worse than 1914, sir, is it not? It is taking longer to get back to work." The Irishman had little to say. He was preoccupied reading the *Daily Star*, and the section engrossing him was not the general news, or the editorial page, or the funnies, or Eaton's advertisements, but—the page devoted to stock market quotations. "Interested?" I asked. He grinned. Out of the darkness came a figure bearing a knapsack. He had just "arrived home" from Calgary, in an empty horse-car, with 13 others. "Bad everywhere you go," he said. "Well, I guess I'll register with the clerk, and sit around the rotunda for awhile before going to bed."

Our next neighbour had built himself a dugout by the railway siding. He was playing a mouth organ as we approached. His "wee hoose" had a bed for two, and his "buddy" was out for the evening. There was an improvised table with a box for a seat. His stock of groceries was in a fruit basket, and consisted of pancake flour and a can of syrup. He had begged a bit of lumber and made a door for the dugout, for upon returning one day they found two not very clean men on their bed, and they had to boil their bed clothing, consisting of a bed-covering and an attenuated mattress, given by a man for whom he had worked. "A man can keep clean," he said. "There is lots of water." A decent, friendly chap, this neighbour of ours.

Guided by a glimmer of light, we found the next camp of three men well kept. They had three individual bivouacs of rushes, built on the thatched roof plan, and bound together by striplings sewn through the thatch. The floors were of rushes. Ventilation is from the back. By means of a chain the back may be opened or closed. The opening is screened by a curtain. These are most ingenious huts. The resourcefulness of these men impressed us greatly. If they had a blanket each, they would be "jake." It gets cold about three in the morning.

Then around an open fire we found fifteen Finlanders and a warm welcome. I sat on the grass beside one of them for a chat. He has been out of work since last autumn. He has a wife and children in Finland. "Hard times," he said. Hope camps open soon. They sleep in boxcars. "Hard bed, put pile up news-papers to make it softer." (Another use for the press.) "How do you know your own boxcar?" "Well, they are numbered, you know." A friendly group of men, glad to have a chat with their neighbours.

We heard singing in the darkness and found another group of men—Canadian, English, Irish, Scotch and Newfoundland—with quite a settlement of little shacks, under the cheerful command of "Captain" Macdonald. They were having a good-bye party to three of their number, and we sat and joined in their singing of "Pack All Your Troubles." Three of their pals were leaving for Calgary and possibly Vancouver. They had not yet ordered their Pullman sleeper! "Good luck, boys," we said, as they stepped out into the darkness, three fine-looking, clean boys. We were invited to have tea and inspect the camp—first the open brazier with roaring fire, and a "wee" oven underneath for the "Sunday roast." One bedroom had a magazine table made of firewood.

Above another bed was the photo of a British army officer, framed. The photo had been found in the dump nearby, then a frame was secured from the same source of supply. A trunk in one of the shacks had also been found in the dump.

Hearing Williams and McCleary address me as "Doctor," one of the boys asked my advice about a festered finger. We had a fine visit with these neighbours. One of them said: "We are not Reds. We, in our class, are as good citizens as any other class, but we are hard up now. When, Doctor, do you think this work will start up. We registered today."

Then we found a group from Poland, with another class of house. "How do you get along when it rains?" "No bad, no rain through the roof." I examined the roof of the lean-to; quite rain-proof. Clothes were hanging on a discarded radio aerial wire found in the dump. The leader of the camp, pointing to it, said: "We got radio wire, see, but no radio." In saying good night, he added: "Englishman in this camp, Irishman, Scottishman, Chinese man, Russian, Polish, Canadian–all brothers. No 'chew the rag.'"

In a dugout, six foot square, we found five boys reading one magazine by the light of a lamp with a broken chimney, also "found in the dump." A few friendly words and we moved on along the stream. A shout of greeting from two of the men having a midnight bathe, then back to the brick-works.

We have probably four hundred neighbours in the Don Valley. They are plain, ordinary folks, "just like you and me," over-come temporarily by unemployment. They did not know who we were, but we were welcomed because we were friendly. We did not hear an oath, and we did not hear a complaint. They did not rail against the government, or against existing conditions. They are eagerly anticipating the opening up of work following the registration now taking place.

There may be bums in this jungle of ours, but they are the exception. Their best friends may say that some of them would just as soon not work, but I know that the vast majority there are men who are used to work and willing to work. They are normal folks, in abnormal circumstances. Theirs is the drab comfort of the jungle, because they have no work for the moment and they have no money.

The men paid tribute to the kindness of the people along the Danforth. I feel like adding a word of appreciation to the Don Valley Brick Company.

We walked through Grange Park on the way home. As I walk through this park each morning to my office, I see frequently many men stretched under the trees and on the benches. Last night we counted over 50 in this comparatively small park, lying on newspapers on the benches and along the fences. I presume the other public parks have their quota.

We must be kind in these difficult days, and understanding and more generous than ever before; and, God helping us, we must seek and find a way to make the jungle an unnecessary part of our civic life. What we saw last night, with all its implications, moved us profoundly. It is not easy to write about it.

Christ, as he gazed upon the city, wept.

## AUTOS FROM DUMPS MADE INTO BUNKS

Another story from the Vancouver *Daily Province.*

By J. Sydney Williamson.

Truly one-half of the world doesn't know how the other half lives, and I doubt if 95 per cent of Vancouver citizens know how the floaters in our midst are living, now that relief has been cut off from so many and the Emergency Refuge on Pender Street has been closed.

Out on False Creek flats there is what is known as a jungle, in the vernacular. Several of them, in fact, scatter around the edges of the flats.

Yesterday I visited the one near the corner of Prior Street and Campbell Avenue, and found more than 100 men sleeping out in makeshift *go-downs* built of materials picked up on an automobile dump nearby.

And these chaps are not all floaters, either. I spoke to one man who said he'd been a resident of Vancouver for 20 years. He had met with ill-luck, lost his job and was unable to find work. He had been cared for by the Emergency Refuge until it closed down, but after that had no other place to sleep than in the jungle.

On the whole these fellows are clean-cut, healthy and willing to do any kind of work. They don't appear to be the obstreperous type, and don't make a fuss. They are making the best of a bad job. There are practically all nationalities there—a few Scotch, English and Irish, Danes, Swedes, Norwegians and a little colony of four or five Chinamen who have two makeshift shacks buried deep in the patch of brush.

You wouldn't know the latter were there, were it not for the sing song of their voices as they chatter away to one another.

Many of the men are returned soldiers who cheerfully did their bit overseas. The general appearance of the jungle, in fact, reminds one of a scene in a ruined village back of the lines, where the Tommies had rigged up shelters of any old material that was lying around handy.

Nearby is a dump which has become a graveyard for old automobiles that have had their day. These wrecks have been put to most ingenious uses. Old car bodies are used as "bunkhouses."

One chap has rigged a shelter for himself out of the bodies of two old Ford cars, one turned upside down on top of the other, with a piece of a canvas top thrown over to keep off the rain.

Some of the lucky ones have found car seats, which they are using for bunks.

Bits of wood, tin, auto bonnets, old signs, scraps of rags and anything handy on the dump have been used to rig up shelters. Most of these men are drifters, it is true, but the majority of necessity and not from choice. They represent all trades: stone-masons, loggers, engineers, mechanics, cooks, and common labourers. But they'll work at anything they can get.

A short time ago this jungle was brought to the attention of Rev. Andrew Roddan, pastor of First United Church, by the police, who asked for his co-operation.

He found these unemployed sleeping out in their make-shift shelters, some of them in the rain. Rats as big as kittens were scurrying round among the sleeping forms, scavenging for any odd scraps of food they might find.

Mr. Roddan investigated for himself, and found many of the men practically starving; some of them so hungry they were for-aging in the garbage of the dump looking for something to eat.

Others of them begged for food downtown, sharing whatever they obtained with their comrades. Mr. Roddan immediately busied himself and, through appeals over the radio, brought the state of affairs to the attention of a number of kind-hearted citizens who have contributed food and money. Every evening he fills his auto with food and takes it down to the jungle to distribute to the men. But it takes a lot to feed such a band of hungry men. Their rations consist of a few spuds, fish, a couple of fat sausages, half a loaf of bread and a little tea, sugar and salt, each day.

There are many similar jungles scattered around the edge of the flats, and another one under Georgia Street Viaduct. Until a few days ago these men were drawing their water from a stag-nant pool of rainwater on the dump. When this condition was brought to the attention of the civic health department by Mr. Roddan, an extension was put in and a stand tap installed at the edge of the jungle.

"I interviewed Hon. Gideon Robertson, federal minister of Labour, when he was in the city recently, and drew his attention to these conditions," said Mr. Roddan, "but he does not seem to be able to grasp the seriousness of the situation. Unless strong pressure is brought to bear on the federal government, it doesn't look as though it were going to do very much to help out."

These are the impressions of some of those who have visited the jungles, and the same story could be told of the situation in other city and railway terminals across Canada. We continue our story at this point.

*Mulligan* is the great dish: a conglomeration of potatoes and meat and whatever is on hand, thrown together in a pot and well cooked and served hot. Filling, if not always palatable.

## ✣ DEMOCRACY ✣

There is a democracy in the jungle that is a stern reality. Here you will find democracy without the *mock*; where the men are all on the level. Each man has to play the game, no stealing or hijacking. No drones are allowed in the jungle, and no bullying. These are some of the unwritten laws which stern necessity compels them to observe; but what a place it is to study human nature. Every bit of information and news is passed around. What the prospects are for work in the East or the West, North or South. How the bulls (policemen) are treating the men on the way. What the chances are on the Main Stem (street) for bumming a meal. Where any work is opening up. Those they have met coming across. The adventures they have had, the hardships they have endured and the prospects for the future.

These are all recited and talked over in the jungles, and now, when the night falls and the stars come out, thousands of these homeless men crawl into their crude shelters, somebody's boys for whom someone cares, but men without a home, without a cause, without a country.

## ✦ ALL IN A DAY'S WORK ✦
### By A. R. Evans.

When it is pleasant to rest from the strenuous business of following aviators and fishermen, engineers and coal miners, I
shall call on the minister of some interesting church. This had
been my thought for some weeks. Now that I have had my day
with a minister, such was my thought no longer—it was not a day
of rest and quietness. No long peaceful hours in the dim religious light of a comfortable study—no protracted discussions of
theology from an armchair. An exploration of the jungles—feeding and clothing hundreds of people—a funeral and two weddings—a period of consultation on domestic problems—and a
journey (voluntary) to the police station. The reader may possibly know now that my day was spent with the Rev. Andrew
Roddan, of First United Church. Here is no day of ease, no day
of union hours, no day of ministerial theorizing—but a long day
of ministerial "doing."

The official day begins in the church office at 9 o'clock.
Having seven children in his household, it is not difficult to sup-
pose that considerable domestic activity has already taken place.
But this, the minister admitted, was only a sideline, again prov-
ing the theory that it is the busy man who has the time. The first
hours of the official day, at least, are generally devoted to the
large number of men who daily gather at this relief centre. I
remember on a former visit a line of over 1,200 men passed
through the church; each man carried away food for the day.
Today, the men are lined up at the door as usual; the line
extends around the church and down the lane. With the passing
of summer, the men are now concerned with the problem of
clothing and boots that will not leak. I have always been impressed
by the extreme orderliness of the men. Even in days of greatest
stress and numbers, no police aid has ever been needed. The

knack of managing large numbers of unemployed must be well known here, because human nature is still–human nature.

The doors are open and the men come in, one at a time, each one a study in human interest. To many natures, such a contact day after day would become insupportably depressing. A sense of humour, a cheery optimism, and a great love of mankind–all are necessary to preserve a normal outlook upon the world.

The record card of each man is examined and he explains his need. As each request is made, it is usually accompanied by a practical demonstration; the cracks in boots are displayed, the lack of socks, holes in trousers, thinness of a coat, no shirt, no hat. If the need is sufficiently apparent an order of the article is given to the applicant. If the need is there, but not actually pressing for the moment, no order can be given; the supply is not equal to all the applicant asks for. Books could be written on the types of human nature daily passing through these church doors. Occasionally some bold, experienced character makes his demand as one to whom the world owes a living. But the great majority of applicants are hesitant, almost apologetic, concerning their misfortunes. Some are almost dazed, not understanding the economic forces that seem to be tossing them about.

The minister cannot stay with this long line of men continually. He is often called to answer the telephone or give friendly counsel to some seeker for the way out of a difficulty. A clinic of advice is carried on intermittently all morning. These difficulties are generally those pertaining to various human relationships, the domestic problem predominating. This phase of the minister's activity is the most responsible of all his many services. To this clinic several thousand men and women bring their problems every year. In the minds of a surprising number of enquirers, the minister is endowed with supernatural powers; he would be a superman indeed to answer all questions. Almost he needs be a fortune-teller to give direct answers to all and sundry.

A mother has two daughters, one entering business, and one a professional. She asks the minister if they will make successes. The minister has not met the daughters and has known the mother only a few minutes. What can he tell her? Not much more than that he hopes they will be successful. A young lady who is about to be married is worried with the thought of promising to "obey." This is one of the easy problems and her mind is soon at rest, at least about that question. Numbers of enquirers ask how they may change their names. Their reasons for this desire are varied—probably to start all over again is the most usual motive. Girls have boyfriends who are this and that and do so and so—should they marry them? The young men have similar problems, and what should they do? Very often the families on one side or the other insist on complicating matters. The judgment of Solomon seems necessary to untangle the mazes of the younger generation. Wives and husbands are "stepping out" on each other; what should be done? Parents have children who refuse to be "managed," and children have parents who stay out all night. One hopeful young bride had found a man she cared for more than her husband; she asked the minister to negotiate the "trade." What a life!

After the clinic we drove down to the Welfare department where the second-hand clothing, boots and blankets are stored. The men who had received orders for supplies earlier in the morning were just being let in. A mass of them surged about the tables and shelves on which are heaped all kinds of clothing. The men pick over piles of coats, socks, boots, hats, trousers, ties, overcoats, sweaters. When they have found the size, colour, weight, or perhaps style that appeals to them they bring the articles to a checking desk along with their signed order. The parcel is wrapped, a value is given to it and the man signs his name, if possible, for his "purchase." Everyone's "charge account" seemed to be good; there was no enquiry by a credit department.

While there is much that is pathetic, there are occasional spots of humour. The sight of so many fine types of young manhood being forced to pick over this motley assortment of garments in a new country like Canada is in itself a matter to give pause. The broken old relics who hulk about the tables are sad enough. They are practically through with life, at least with the useful part of it; even in times of prosperity they would have no economic value. They seem for the most part resigned and sometimes stolid. But the young men who are worried, confused and sometimes frightened—they are the saddest element of the whole situation. They are caught up by forces they are almost powerless to combat. They have possibly long lives before them, they are frightened by the broken wrecks all around them—clearly, they don't know just what to do. When ambition is lost they are all through.

But the touches of humour are there too. Clothing is put on which is of such grotesque misfit that even the men themselves can smile. Colours clash and nobody cares. Is the thing warm, will it keep out the rain? That is the main question. There is an interesting coincidence this morning. Three years ago a one-legged man left one new shoe which he could not use. Now another one-legged man appears three years later who needs a shoe for the other foot. We all watch breathlessly while he tries it on—and it fits! Who wouldn't believe in Santa Claus?

In the midst of all this scurrying for "bargains" the minister must rush back to the church. The hour of a wedding has arrived, and so we drive back. The two are already waiting, several young friends stand together in a group in obvious embarrassment. They seem uncertain whether to mourn or rejoice; evidently they have never been married themselves. Weddings in this church are not often a profitable sideline. In this case the minister has paid for the license himself. The groom began to fear that, as a single man, he would never find employment. He felt that marriage would bring him a step nearer the elusive job, even if temporary. He was like a man breaking a window to enjoy the comforts of jail. He had not the philosophy of Hamlet; he was willing to "fly evils that he knew not of." However, thousands of couples are married for worse reasons. What a life! None of the usual trappings of a wedding was in evidence. Two of the friends had rather pathetic bags of confetti, attempting by a little colour to add a festive air to the occasion. There is at least one redeeming feature about a wedding of this type: there are no elaborate details in the paper next day. "The bride was lovely in a gown of white flat crepe with lace jacquette. Her embroidered net veil, which fell to the floor was held in place with clusters of orange blossoms. She carried a shower bouquet of Ophelia roses and Lily of the Valley. She had a mohair picture hat, etc., etc." You know the rest with your eyes shut.

After this wedding we went to an upper study to look over the photos for a book, *God in the Jungles*, which the pastor had just finished. Those who toured the jungles last summer would be familiar with some of the refuges and refugees. I could not but marvel at the fact of a book finished in the odd moment of overflowing days. How many of us plan to write our book "someday" when we have a comfortable studio, and months of time, and the weather is just right, and we have a fine sharp pencil, and stacks of perfect paper, and, of course, "if we feel like it." But here is a book done in spite of the stress of long days and countless demands. And let me tell you about something else. On an easel by the window is a large painting, also just finished, a combination of mountains, sea and forest, such as we have along our BC coast. I know nothing about pictures except that I sometimes like them. I liked this one. I expect that critics could say technical things about it, just as they do about the music ordinary people enjoy. There were other smaller landscapes of familiar scenes all done by the versatile minister himself. When the cares of a great mission church press in too hard on the mind, then it is necessary to withdraw for a brief space–to dwell apart–to make dreams come true.

Almost all successfully busy men have a hobby; they are too busy not to have one. It has psychological justification. By this time I expected almost anything–a concealed pipe organ, played by the pastor; a manuscript translated from the Hindi; and an opera in process of composition–anything seemed possible after the book and the painting. Whatever the remaining surprises of the minister's study, they must be left behind; we have just time for a quick inspection of the church kindergarten. The pastor calls this department the League of Nations. Here were miniature representatives of 14 different nationalities. It seemed to me Orientals headed the list–and how they all looked just alike! I marvelled that the teacher could call them by name. There are 27 different nationalities under the care of this church. How many Vancouver people know the crowded East End?

When we are back in the church office again, a young man of about 20 is waiting to speak with the pastor. They have a short conversation and the boy goes out. He has just been released from jail; this is his first day out. He is sent to the John Howard Society for the rehabilitation of released prisoners. If he needs clothing he comes to the church. If he needs work a Howard official helps him. Between the two organizations many a released prisoner finds himself again. Not quite every man's hand is against him, as he often believes. Every Sunday in the congregation of First United are numbers of former prisoners. It would be possible, but perhaps not wise to mention positions filled in this church by released men. The great point is they have stayed with the church that helped them in their darkest hour.

At this point in the day's activities there is a hurried drive to the police court. These visits of the pastor on behalf of some accused person happen several times every week. There is no attempt to obtain the release of guilty persons worthy of sentence. But often, especially in the case of younger culprits, it is possible for the minister to present an angle of the case unknown or overlooked by a lawyer or officer. Former conduct, home surroundings, poverty, special motives—these, presented in a sympathetic way, often throw an unsuspected light on the case and bring a suspension or a mitigation of sentences. The pastor was very emphatic in his statement that all officers and policemen had been very ready with their co-operation. It was often expressed as a wish of the officials that other citizens of the city would take an active interest in the work of the force. The work of the police in the East End has undoubtedly been made easier by the establishment of First United and its many activities.

Throughout the day there has seemed to be just time to go from one appointment to another. Probably the smooth working of appointments has been made possible by an efficient secretary. From the police court there is just the right amount of time to reach a funeral. A funeral among the very poor is always most pathetic. In the household of the bereaved well-to-do, so many expedients are possible to alleviate the circumstances of grief— travel, books, music, friends tend to occupy the mind and divert the thought. But the poor must return to the same rooms, live almost the same life as before, be circumscribed by the same monotony of toil. While listening to the simple service for a child, I thought of a fragment of Sandburg's poem, "The Right to Grief." He is describing the funeral of the daughter of an extremely poor stockyard labourer.

Now his three-year-old daughter
Is in a white coffin that cost him a week's wages.
Every Saturday night he will pay the undertaker fifty cents till the
    debt is wiped out.
The hunky and his wife and the kids

Cry over the pinched face almost at peace in the white box.
They remember it was scrawny and ran up high doctor bills.
They are glad it is gone for the rest of the family now will have
more to eat and wear.

There is much more, but that is enough. It is enough to show the stark realities of life, which, without gloss, tend to be a bit unpleasant, even startling. On the return to the church office once again, still more visitors were gathered waiting for interviews. Last month 737 visitors came to this same office. Such a stream of visitors must carry away something worthwhile, or it would diminish; but the stream grows greater. It will be at least 7:30 before the last caller has left. Then the minister may be able to go home. Perhaps not; there is a meeting somewhere this evening to be addressed, perhaps at eleven he may be home. Once at home, there is an accumulation of telephone calls to be answered. The phone still keeps ringing. Sometimes it rings till 2 o'clock. Let it ring! Even a minister is not inexhaustible.

So that is a day with a minister—at least it is the day of Rev. Andrew Roddan. Not only are there six days of unceasing activity, but seven—and the seventh is even more strenuous than the others. The seventh is a day of speaking, morning and evening, and the evening service repeated to accommodate the overflowing congregations. An audience of 50,000 radio listeners form a part of the adherents of the First Church.

How would you like to trade your eight-hour day for one like this?

## ✣ SUPPOSE NOBODY CARED ✣

In the story of the Good Samaritan, Jesus reveals the very heart of the Gospel. He sums it all up in these three words: "He had compassion." Undoubtedly this story has been the mainspring, directly and indirectly, for all true works of mercy, philanthropy, and fraternity. Jesus was a Master in the art of word-painting and He has fixed this picture indelibly on the mind of man. Would to God that our actions would equal our knowledge in our dealings with our fellow men. Nobody cared for this unfortunate man left lying in the ditch, bleeding, naked and, to all appearances, dead. Even the priest, the champion of religion, when he drew near, looked at him, but as he did not feel any sense of obligation to lend a hand, he passed by on the other side. The Levite stopped his singing for a moment when he saw the situation, but as the man did not belong to his race or religion, it did not take him long to make up his mind that this was none of his business, and he passed by on the other side.

But (I want you to notice how much depends on that little word *but*) when the Samaritan saw him he had compassion; he cared. We have reason to thank God for that long line of noble, self-sacrificing men and women who have cared for their less fortunate brothers and sisters. One night, while I was addressing several hundred of these homeless men, one of them shouted out, "What is the difference between Christianity and religion?" I said: "All the difference in the world, my friend. A man may be as full of religion as an egg is full of food and not have the spirit of Christ in him." Religion without compassion is the coldest thing under Heaven. In the name of religion men have done some hellish things in this world, as history clearly reveals.

Religion has sometimes expressed that spirit that Robert Burns had in mind when he said: "Man's inhumanity to man, makes countless thousands mourn." The church has so often forgotten that man has a body to be cared for as well as a soul to be saved and that the two must have proper and careful attention. It is only when men have had the true spirit of Christ in them that they have turned aside from their selfishness and indifference to lend a helping hand among the underprivileged and less fortunate members of society.

The complete message of Jesus takes into consideration man's temporal as well as his spiritual needs. "What does it profit," asks the Apostle James, "if a man say he hath works? Can that faith save him? If a brother or sister be naked, and in lack of daily food, and one of you say unto them, 'Go in peace, be ye warmed and filled,' and yet ye give them not the things needful to the body; what doth it profit? Even so faith, if it have not works, is dead in itself."

There are some Christians who hold the pilgrim theory of life and that fits in with their theology. It finds expression in the idea that the world is bad, and going to the dogs; therefore our duty is to get through it as quickly as possible and all the while keep our eye on the pie in the sky.

Can you imagine anything further from the mind of Jesus than that conception of life? This philosophy fitted in with the Pharisees' conception of religion. They could pass by the poor beggars in the street with the dogs licking their festering sores; they could say their prayers, go to church. Jesus said: "You must face your duty to God and learn to love your neighbour as yourself."

There is another theory that prevails, the practical view of life. It teaches that we are here for a purpose and there is a work to be done. There are thousands of our fellows who are living in sin. There are those who have lost the way. Some are in rebellion, some are sad, and some are hopeless, and it is our task in the spirit of the Master, not only to rescue the brands from the burning, but as soon as possible to put out the fires which would destroy their lives. What a difference it makes when we care as Jesus cared. He never could look at a group of people but His heart was moved with compassion; He cared. When the Apostle Paul caught the spirit of Jesus, he went out, not caring for himself, but filled with a great zeal and love to be of service to his

Master so that he was ready to die for Him. Down through the centuries of time men have caught that vision and have followed the gleam. This is the spirit that has lifted this old world nearer to Heaven because somebody cared.

It is true in the experience of the missionaries of the Cross, in the experience of St. Patrick, St. Mungo and St. Andrew and Francis of Assisi. We have this spirit exemplified in the life of Hudson Taylor, William Cary, Dr. [Wilfred] Grenfell, David Livingstone and Mary Slessor. The great preachers of history, St. Peter, Savonarola, John Knox, John Wesley, [Charles] Spurgeon and [Henry Ward] Beecher, or in the lives of the great reformers like Abraham Lincoln, John Bright, [Richard] Cobden and [William] Wilberforce. They all cared.

When Charles Dickens saw the conditions in the prisons, workhouses, schools and factories of his day, he said, "I care," and he awakened the public conscience to its duty. Lord Shaftsbury, after long hours in the House of Parliament, took his lantern and went down under the bridges and along the highways and byways and gathered in the homeless men and boys, because, he said, "I care."

When Florence Nightingale heard of the sufferings of the British soldiers in the Crimea, she said: "I care," and she went out and rendered a great service, so that when this Angel of Mercy passed the long rows of wounded soldiers they turned and kissed her shadow as it fell upon their beds.

It was this spirit that stirred the heart of William Booth when he realized the need in darkest England among the poor people of his day. He said, "I care." When John Howard saw the life of the prisoners in England and on the Continent he said, "I care. I want to spend the rest of my life helping my unfortunate brothers and sisters, I care." When Edith Cavell faced the guns of her executioners she said, "Patriotism is not enough; I care."

This is the spirit which has blessed the world, helped to keep it sweet, revealed the spirit of the Master and prevented it from falling into gross selfishness and sin.

What is compassion? Simply, it is that something of the eternal which goes out from us towards suffering humanity. This is what the world needs today. We have had an overflow of nationalism, commercialism, science, and education. Now the time has come for an overflow of compassion and goodwill.

> Not what we have, but what we share,
> For the gift without the giver is bare;
> Who gives himself with his alms feed three—
> Himself, his hungering neighbour and me.

We can never improve the play by changing the scenery. It is spiritual determinism that ultimately determines all things, and we must aim for that ideal. When we get men to put Christ first, we will take a great step forward to that day when the new world order will be ushered in. An order in which the motive of service and mutual helpfulness will take the place of selfish, heartless, cruel competition which is so rampant in the world today.

It is in this spirit and by this power that the problem of the homeless man can and must be solved.

> Christ claims our help in many a strange disguise;
> Now, fever ridden, on a bed he lies;
> Homeless he wanders, now beneath the stars;
> Now counts the number of his prison bars;
> Now bends beside us, crowned with hoary hairs,
> No need have we to climb the heavenly stairs,
> And press our kisses on His feet and hands;
> In every man that suffers, He, the Man of Sorrows, stands!